# ROMAN HOLIDAY

## Ian McLellan Hunter

**Level 2**
(1300-word)

Retold by Nina Wegner

IBC パブリッシング

## はじめに

　ラダーシリーズは、「はしご (ladder)」を使って一歩一歩上を目指すように、学習者の実力に合わせ、無理なくステップアップできるよう開発された英文リーダーのシリーズです。

　リーディング力をつけるためには、繰り返したくさん読むこと、いわゆる「多読」がもっとも効果的な学習法であると言われています。多読では、「1. 速く 2. 訳さず英語のまま 3. なるべく辞書を使わず」に読むことが大切です。スピードを計るなど、速く読むよう心がけましょう（たとえば TOEIC® テストの音声スピードはおよそ1分間に150語です）。そして1語ずつ訳すのではなく、英語を英語のまま理解するくせをつけるようにします。こうして読み続けるうちに語感がついてきて、だんだんと英語が理解できるようになるのです。まずは、ラダーシリーズの中からあなたのレベルに合った本を選び、少しずつ英文に慣れ親しんでください。たくさんの本を手にとるうちに、英文書がすらすら読めるようになってくるはずです。

《**本シリーズの特徴**》
- 中学校レベルから中級者レベルまで5段階に分かれています。自分に合ったレベルからスタートしてください。
- クラシックから現代文学、ノンフィクション、ビジネスと幅広いジャンルを扱っています。あなたの興味に合わせてタイトルを選べます。
- 巻末のワードリストで、いつでもどこでも単語の意味を確認できます。レベル1、2では、文中の全ての単語が、レベル3以上は中学校レベル外の単語が掲載されています。
- カバーにヘッドホーンマークのついているタイトルは、オーディオ・サポートがあります。ウェブから購入/ダウンロードし、リスニング教材としても併用できます。

《**使用語彙について**》
レベル1:中学校で学習する単語約1000語
レベル2:レベル1の単語+使用頻度の高い単語約300語
レベル3:レベル1の単語+使用頻度の高い単語約600語
レベル4:レベル1の単語+使用頻度の高い単語約1000語
レベル5:語彙制限なし

# Contents

*Chapter 1*
The Princess ...... 3

*Chapter 2*
A Gentlemen's Agreement ...... 14

*Chapter 3*
Anya Around Town ...... 22

*Chapter 4*
The Three Friends ...... 36

*Chapter 5*
Seeing Rome ...... 42

*Chapter 6*
The Dance at the River ...... 51

*Chapter 7*
Two Hearts ...... 61

*Chapter 8*
The Last Meeting ...... 70

Word List ...... 86

## 【読み始める前に】

本文中に出てくるキーワードです。はじめに目を通しておくとよいでしょう。さらに詳しく知りたい方は巻末の辞書を参照してください。

- [ ] applaud
- [ ] calm
- [ ] carve
- [ ] countess
- [ ] dizzy
- [ ] embassy
- [ ] front-page
- [ ] grab
- [ ] greet
- [ ] lean
- [ ] pour
- [ ] rub
- [ ] ruin
- [ ] sidewalk
- [ ] uneasy
- [ ] yell

## 登場人物紹介

**Princess Ann** アン王女　某小国の王女。ヨーロッパ各国を親善訪問中。王女ということを隠してローマの街を歩き回るときはAnya Smithと名乗る

**Dr. Bonnachoven** バンノックホーベン医師　王女付きの侍医。神経の高ぶっている王女に眠りやすくなる注射を打つ

**Joe Bradley** ジョー・ブラッドレイ　アメリカ人新聞記者。ひょんなことから王女のローマ観光につき合うことになる

**Irving Radovich** アービング・ラドビッチ　ジョーの友人のカメラマン

**Mr. Hennessy** ヘネシー氏　ジョーのボス

**Mario Delani** マリオ・デラニ　王女の髪を切った床屋

## 物語に出てくるローマ市内スポット

**Spanish Steps** スペイン階段　スペイン広場にある階段。アンはここでアイスクリームを食べる。

**Mouth of Truth** 真実の口　警察に嘘をついた後にジョーがアンを連れて行く。嘘つきがこの口の中に手を入れると噛まれるという言い伝えがある。

**River Saint Angelo** サンタンジェロ河　船上ダンスが行われる川。映画では、テヴェレ川でこのシーンが撮影された。

**Piazza Venezia** ヴェネツィア広場　アンとジョーがスクーターに乗って、この辺りを走った。

**Coliseum** コロッセオ　スクーターで最初に訪れる場所、巨大な円形闘技場。

# ROMAN HOLIDAY

CHAPTER *1*
# *The Princess*

Princess Ann was all over the news. She was traveling through Europe. But this was not a holiday for the princess. No, this was work. She met with kings and queens to build strong friendships for her country. First, she visited London, then Amsterdam, then Paris, and then it was on to Rome.

In Rome, she was the special guest at a ball. Important people came from all over the world to meet her. She was polite to everyone and danced all night. But she was glad when the ball ended and she was finally allowed to go to her room.

"Here is your milk to help you sleep," said the countess, as Ann got ready for bed. The countess was in charge of taking care of Ann.

Ann stood on her bed and looked out the window. There was music playing outside.

"I hate this nightgown," Ann said. "And I hate all my underwear, too. They make me feel like I'm two hundred years old. I wish I could join those young people dancing outside."

"Please get into bed," the countess said. "And let me tell you what you're doing tomorrow."

The countess read a long list of visits and meetings Ann had the next day. Ann felt herself getting dizzy thinking of all the work she had to do.

## Chapter 1: The Princess

"Stop! Please stop!" Ann cried out in the middle of the countess's list.

"Are you ill, Ann?" asked the countess. "Let me call Doctor Bonnachoven."

"I don't want to see the doctor! And it's no use, because I'll be dead before the doctor gets here!" Ann cried. She was being rather difficult.

"You're not going to die, Ann," said the countess.

Doctor Bonnachoven came quickly and found Ann lying still with her eyes closed.

"Are you asleep, princess?" The doctor asked.

"No!" said Ann.

"It's very important that she is well and happy for her meetings tomorrow," the countess said.

"Well this will only take a minute," the doctor said. He took Ann's temperature and looked her over. Everything was fine.

"I'm sorry, Doctor Bonnachoven. I promise I'll be well tomorrow. I'll smile and be polite and build good trade relations and be in the news and...and..." Ann started to cry, feeling dizzy again.

"Here, this will help you sleep," the doctor said. He gave her a shot.

"What is it?" Ann asked.

"It's a new medicine that will help you feel happy," the doctor said. "And the best thing to do right now is to do exactly what you want." He packed up his things and told Ann and the countess good night.

When the doctor and countess left the room, Ann sat up in bed. She looked out the window again at the young people dancing outside. With a smile, she changed into some simple clothes. She left her room very quietly and walked out to the garden.

Chapter 1: The Princess

Ann found a little truck parked in the garden. She climbed into the back and hid between some boxes. Soon, the driver came to the truck, got in, and drove to the gate. Ann felt sleepy but she was excited for what was about to happen. The guards at the gate let the truck out into the city. All of a sudden, Ann was free!

Ann smiled and leaned against the boxes. The truck passed a restaurant filled with people. Then it passed a couple riding a scooter. Ann waved and the couple waved back. For a moment, the truck stopped, and Ann jumped out. As she walked, she passed the window of a room on the second story of a building.

Inside that room sat Joe Bradley, Irving Radovich, and some other men. They were playing cards and betting money. Irving was winning.

"After this last game, you gentlemen have to go home," Irving said. "I have an early meeting with the princess tomorrow. I'm taking her picture."

"Early?" said Joe Bradley. "My invitation from the princess says 11:45 a.m. That's not early at all."

"Irving is just afraid of losing the money that he won tonight," said a card player. "Right, Irv?"

"That's right," said Irving with a smile.

"Well, that's fine with me," said Joe. "I don't have much money left, so I'll go home now. See you tomorrow at the princess's little party, Irv. Good night, gentlemen."

As Joe walked down the street, he noticed a young girl lying on a park bench. He slowed down.

"So happy," said Ann. The medicine the doctor gave her was working—but maybe it

## Chapter 1: The Princess

was working a little too much. She sounded drunk, and she smiled with her eyes closed. Joe was going to keep on walking, but Ann almost fell off the bench.

"Hey! Hey! Wake up!" said Joe, catching her and making her sit up.

"Thank you very much, delighted," said Ann in her princess voice.

"Wake up," said Joe.

"No, thank you," said Ann. "You may sit down."

"I think you better sit up. You are too young to get picked up by the police."

"Two-thirty, and back here to change. Two forty-five, meeting with the minister," said Ann, listing the things she had to do the next day.

"You know, a young girl like you shouldn't drink liquor," said Joe.

Just then, Joe heard a taxi coming up the

road. He waved at it and the taxi stopped.

"Look here," said Joe to the girl. "Here's a taxi. He'll take you home."

"Mmmm," said Ann. "So happy."

Joe helped her into the taxi.

"Tell the driver where you need to go. Do you have money?"

"Never carry money," Ann said.

"Fine, I'll pay for you," said Joe. He got into the car next to her. "Where do you live?"

Ann was falling back asleep. Joe tried to wake her, but her head just rolled from side to side and she smiled with her eyes closed. This was a lot of trouble, and Joe didn't want any of it. But what could he do?

"Fine," he said. He gave the driver his own address.

When the taxi arrived at Joe's house, Joe tried to wake the girl again.

## Chapter 1: The Princess

"Hey, wake up. This is my house, but I gave the driver more money. Just tell him where you live and he will take you home. Good bye," Joe said and walked away.

The driver took one look at Ann sleeping and called after Joe.

"Oh, no! Sir, my taxi is not for sleeping! I have to go home too! She can't stay in my taxi!"

"I don't even know this girl!" Joe tried to explain. "She is not my problem!" But the taxi driver would not take her, so Joe gave up.

"All right," Joe said, pulling Ann out of the car. The taxi quickly drove away. Joe opened his door and helped her in. Ann was half sleeping and half walking. He had to help her up the steps and into his small room.

"Is this the closet?" Ann asked when they were inside.

"No!" said Joe. His feelings were a little hurt. "This is my room."

"Mmm... So happy," Ann said.

"Well, here are some pajamas. You can sleep there on the couch," Joe said.

"This is very strange," Ann said. "I have never been alone with a man before. But I don't seem to mind it." She began to take off her shirt.

"Um, well, I think I'll step out for some coffee," Joe said.

"You may go now," Ann said.

"Yeah, thanks a lot," said Joe as he left.

Back at the embassy, the countess, the general, and the ambassador all sat around a desk. They were all in their night clothes. A guard entered the room and said, "We cannot find her, sir."

"Did you search the garden?" asked the ambassador.

## Chapter 1: The Princess

"Yes, every inch of it," said the guard.

"I see. Then you must promise that you won't talk about this to anyone. The princess is missing, but this is top secret. Will you promise?" said the ambassador.

"Yes, sir. I promise."

"Thank you. You may go," said the ambassador. The guard left the room.

Alone again, the countess, the general, and the ambassador looked at each other. Their eyes were filled with worry.

## Chapter 2
# *A Gentlemen's Agreement*

The next morning, the top stories in all the newspapers were about the princess. "Princess Ann Suddenly Falls Ill: All Meetings Canceled," the papers read.

Joe woke up when the clock struck noon. Shocked, he looked again at the clock on his desk and hurried out of bed.

"Oh no! The princess interview!" he cried out.

"Hmm?" said Ann, who was still sleeping on the small couch.

## Chapter 2: A Gentlemen's Agreement

Without answering, Joe got dressed and rushed out the door.

Joe arrived at the newspaper office as Mr. Hennessy, his boss, finished reading the morning newspapers.

"Good morning, Joe," said the secretary as Joe entered the office.

"Hello, honey," said Joe. He took the cup of coffee she held in her hand and drank.

"Mr. Hennessy has been looking for you," said the secretary.

"Oh, no," said Joe. He took a piece of bread from her desk. He ate it as he went to Mr. Hennessy's closed door.

"Come in!" said Mr. Hennessy. He sounded very angry.

Joe and the secretary shared worried looks before Joe opened the door and went in.

Mr. Hennessy sat behind his desk in his office.

"Were you looking for me?" asked Joe.

"You're late," Mr. Hennessy said. "We are supposed to come to work at 8:30 a.m. in this office."

"But I've already done my work for the day," said Joe.

"Which was?" asked Mr. Hennessy.

"The interview with the princess at 11:45 a.m."

"And you're already done?" asked Mr. Hennessy, surprised.

"Yes, sir. I got the whole story."

"Well, please excuse me then. I'm sorry."

"It's ok," said Joe, getting up. He was in a hurry to leave.

"But wait just a minute," said Mr. Hennessy. "This is very interesting. Tell me about the interview." Mr. Hennessy looked at the morning newspapers on his desk.

"Well, it wasn't so special, really," said Joe.

## Chapter 2: A Gentlemen's Agreement

"I don't have much to tell you."

"But did she answer all the questions? What did she say about the future of Europe?"

"Um, well," said Joe, "she said it was fine."

"Fine?"

"Just fine."

"Right. What did she say about the future friendship of nations?"

"Um," said Joe, looking at his feet.

"Well?" said Mr. Hennessy. He crossed his arms, waiting for an answer.

"Children," said Joe. "She said children hold the key to the future."

"Well, Joe, you must have worked very hard to get these answers from the princess!" said Mr. Hennessy. "Especially because she fell ill at 3 a.m. this morning and has canceled all meetings and interviews today!"

Mr. Hennessy threw a newspaper at Joe.

"If you ever woke up on time and read the morning news, you would know this!" Mr. Hennessy yelled. "But instead, you come into my office late and lie!"

Joe looked at the newspaper in front of him. "Oh," was all he could say. Then he saw the picture of the princess in the newspaper. Joe's eyes almost jumped out of his head. It was her! That strange girl that he helped last night!

In the picture, the princess wore a rich, beautiful dress and a diamond crown. But it was the same woman whom Joe had met last night. Princess Ann was sleeping in his room at that very moment. Suddenly, Joe had a great idea.

"Mr. Hennessy," said Joe, "how much would a real interview with the princess be worth?"

## Chapter 2: A Gentlemen's Agreement

"What do you mean?" said Mr. Hennessy, still angry.

"I mean a special interview with the princess. I mean an interview where she talks about more than just the future of nations. If the princess talked about her private life, her loves, her hopes, and her dreams, how much would you pay?" said Joe.

"Why do you care?" Mr. Hennessy asked. "You don't know how to get an interview like that."

"Please, just answer the question," said Joe. "How much?"

Mr. Hennessy threw up his hands, giving up. There was no way to argue with Joe Bradley.

"Oh, something that good would be worth about five thousand dollars at any newspaper," Mr. Hennessy said. "But how would anybody get that interview? The princess is sick!"

"I have a way. I will get that interview, but you have to pay me five thousand dollars. Will you agree to it? If so, shake my hand," said Joe, very excited.

Mr. Hennessy laughed as he shook Joe's hand. It all seemed like a big joke to him.

"Do you realize the princess is sick today and she leaves for Athens tomorrow?" asked Mr. Hennessy.

"Sure I do," said Joe, hurrying to leave the room and get to work.

"Wait just a minute," said Mr. Hennessy. "I want to make another bet with you. If you don't get an interview with the princess at all, you owe me five hundred dollars. Is that a deal?"

"Yes!" said Joe. He shook Mr. Hennessy's hand again. "But I'm going to win this bet. And when you pay me five thousand dollars, I'm going to leave this place. I will buy

Chapter 2: A Gentlemen's Agreement

myself a one-way ticket back home to New York!"

Joe put the newspaper into his pocket and walked out of Mr. Hennessy's office.

CHAPTER 3
## *Anya Around Town*

Back at his apartment, Joe entered his room slowly and quietly. He didn't want to wake the princess. He walked over to the couch, where the princess was still sleeping, dressed in his pajamas. He took out the newspaper and put the picture next to her face. It was her.

"Your Highness?" Joe said, just to make sure. "Your Royal Highness?"

"Mmmm," Ann said. She moved a little with her eyes still closed. "Yes, what is it?"

## Chapter 3: Anya Around Town

Joe smiled wide. Yes, it was her, no doubt about it. Joe carefully picked her up—blankets and all—and placed her on his bed.

"Doctor Bonnachoven," said Ann, still half asleep. "I had so many dreams last night."

"Oh?" said Joe.

"I dreamed... I dreamed that I was sleeping on the street..." said Ann.

"And?"

"And a young man came along... He was tall and strong..."

"And?"

"And he was so mean to me," said Ann, making a face. But then she smiled. "It was so wonderful!" Ann finally opened her eyes. Seeing where she was, she sat up quickly in bed. She held her blankets close to her.

"Good morning!" said Joe.

"You're not Doctor Bonnachoven!" said Ann.

"Who?" said Joe. "I don't know anybody by that name."

"But wasn't I talking to him just now?" asked Ann, looking very worried.

"No, I'm afraid not," lied Joe.

"Am...Am I hurt?" asked Ann, feeling her body under the blanket. She looked at the pajamas she was wearing.

"No, no, you're just fine!" said Joe.

"Would you be so kind as to tell me where I am?"

"This little place is my apartment."

Ann looked even more worried.

"Did you force me to come here?" she asked.

"No, no!" said Joe. "In fact, last night I didn't want you to come here at all."

"Then I have been here all night?"

## Chapter 3: Anya Around Town

"Yes."

"So I spent the night with you?" asked Ann.

"Well, in a way... In separate beds, of course." Now it was Joe's turn to look uneasy.

Ann looked hard at Joe. She decided to believe him, and she suddenly laughed. She held out her hand to him.

"How do you do?" said Ann. "What is your name?"

"How do you do?" said Joe, shaking her hand. "My name is Joe. Joe Bradley."

"It's very nice to meet you. You may sit down," Ann said.

"Thank you. And what is your name?" Joe asked.

"You may call me... Anya. Could you please tell me what time it is?"

"Oh, about one thirty."

"One thirty!" Ann jumped out of bed and went toward the door. "I must get dressed and go!"

"Why do you need to hurry?" asked Joe. "There's lots of time."

"Oh, no! There isn't!" said Ann. "There's so much I have to do today!"

"Here, you can take a bath and get ready. The bathroom is just right here." Joe went into the bathroom and turned on the water for the bath. Ann walked in, still covering herself with her blanket.

"Thank you," she said. She shut the door behind her.

As soon as Ann shut the bathroom door, Joe ran downstairs to the telephone and called Irving Radovich.

Irving was photographing a beautiful model at his home when Joe called.

"Irving! It's Joe. Listen, Irv, can you come

## Chapter 3: Anya Around Town

to my place in about five minutes?" said Joe.

"Joe, I'm in the middle of something right now," said Irving. He looked at the model and she blew a kiss at him. Irving smiled. "I really can't go anywhere."

"Look, Irving, I have something really important I need your help on. I can't tell you right now. There are too many people around me and I don't want them to hear," said Joe. "Please, just come. I'm writing a front-page story for the newspaper and I have to have pictures for it!"

"I'm sorry, Joe, but I'm busy. And I'm meeting Francesca at Rocca's in half an hour—"

Just then Joe heard a scream come from his apartment. He threw down the phone and ran up the stairs.

Joe found Ann in a bath towel facing his cleaning lady.

"That woman just walked into the bathroom!" said Ann.

"Oh, she's my cleaning lady. Please excuse her," said Joe. He held the cleaning lady by the arm and walked her out of the apartment. He told her to come back later. When Joe came back into the apartment, Ann was dressed and standing on the balcony. She looked down at the city below.

"Look at all the people down there! It must be fun to live in a city like this," said Ann. "But really, I have to go now. Thank you for everything."

"Oh! You don't have to go yet!" said Joe.

"I must go. I don't have time to stay," said Ann.

"Well, I'll go with you," said Joe.

"No, thank you. I can find my way alone," said Ann. Joe walked her to the door. Suddenly, she turned to face him.

## Chapter 3: Anya Around Town

"I'm sorry," said Ann, "but may I borrow some money?"

"I remember from last night. You never carry any money, do you?" said Joe.

"No," said Ann, a little shy. "I'm afraid not."

"Sure. Here you are," said Joe. He handed her a thousand lira.

"I promise to pay you back. I will send it to your address," said Ann. "Thank you again, Joe Bradley. Good bye."

"Good bye," said Joe. He shut the door. Then he ran to his window to watch her come out from his building.

Ann soon came out onto the street. She stopped for a moment. She did not quite know where to go. Then she chose a direction and started walking. At first, she seemed a little afraid of the busy people and action all around her. But she soon started to enjoy herself.

When Ann started walking, Joe left his apartment. He ran out to the street. He followed behind Ann, watching her all the time.

Ann walked past shops, looking into the windows and smiling. She stopped at one shop and walked in. It was a barber's shop. Joe walked over to the shop and looked in through the window. He watched Ann as she sat down. She told the barber how short she wanted her hair.

"Like this," said Ann, pulling her long hair up to her shoulders.

## Chapter 3: Anya Around Town

"So short?" asked the Italian barber.

"Yes. Cut it all off," said Ann.

When the barber was done, Ann looked pleased. Her hair was much shorter.

"You are very beautiful. This short hair looks very nice on you," said the barber.

"Thank you," said Ann. She paid him.

"Would you like to come dancing with me tonight?" asked the barber. "The dance is by the river. There will be music and moonlight. It will be very nice!"

"That sounds very nice. I wish I could, but I can't," said Ann. "Good bye!"

Ann walked out of the shop. Joe looked the other way and covered his face with his hand, hiding himself. Ann did not notice him.

"Thank you!" said Ann to the barber as she walked away.

"If you change your mind, the dance is at the river Saint Angelo. Nine o'clock. I'll be there!" the barber called after her.

Next, Ann walked into a shoe shop. She tried on a pair of shoes and bought them. Then she walked toward a man selling ice cream. Joe kept following her. She bought an ice cream and walked to the famous Spanish Steps. Joe watched her from behind a cart selling fruit.

Ann sat down on a step and ate her ice cream. She watched

## Chapter 3: Anya Around Town

the people walking past her, enjoying her time in the city. Joe decided this was his chance.

Joe walked out from behind the cart. He acted as if he were just enjoying a walk in the city. As he walked past Ann, he looked down as if he were seeing her for the first time.

"Well!" said Joe, acting surprised. "It's you again!"

Ann looked up at him and smiled.

"Hello, Joe Bradley!" she said.

"Did you get your hair cut?" asked Joe. "You look so different!"

"Yes, do you like it?"

"Very much. Is that why you were in such a hurry to leave this morning? You had to get your hair cut?" asked Joe.

"No, I...I'm sorry, I should tell you something," said Ann.

"What is it?" asked Joe.

"I ran away from...from school last night," said Ann. "I only meant to leave for an hour or two. But they gave me some medicine that made me fall asleep."

"Ah, I see," said Joe.

"Anyway, I should get back to school," said Ann.

"Well, before you go back why don't you take some time for yourself?" said Joe.

"I would really like to. Maybe for just another hour," said Ann.

"An hour? Why not take the whole day?" pushed Joe.

"I could do all the things I have always wanted to do!" said Ann.

"Like what?"

"Oh, lots of things!" said Ann. "I would like to sit at a sidewalk restaurant, and look in shop windows, and walk in the rain!"

## Chapter 3: Anya Around Town

Joe looked up at the perfectly blue sky. He doubted it would rain today.

"I want to have fun," said Ann. "I want to have a little excitement. I guess that doesn't sound like much to you, does it?"

"It sounds great! Why don't we do all those things together?" asked Joe.

"But don't you have to go to work?" asked Ann.

"Work? No! We will make today a holiday! Your first wish is to go to a sidewalk restaurant, right? I know a great one. It's called Rocca's."

Chapter 4
# *The Three Friends*

Ann and Joe walked to Rocca's and sat at a table. Ann watched the traffic go by. Joe ordered champagne to drink. As they sat, Joe saw Irving walk into the restaurant.

"Irving!" said Joe, walking over to his friend. "I'm glad to see you! Come join us."

Irving sat down at Ann and Joe's table.

"Anya, this is my very good friend, Irving Radovich. Irving, this is Anya," said Joe.

"Anya...?" asked Irving, shaking her hand.

## Chapter 4: The Three Friends

"Smith," said Ann.

"Well, hello Smithy," joked Irving. Ann laughed. She liked her new name.

Irving started to say, "Has anybody told you that you look just like—" but just then Joe kicked him under the table.

"Ow!" said Irving. Thinking that Joe wanted him gone, Irving got up to go.

"Well, I should be going," said Irving.

"Oh, don't go yet!" said Joe, sitting his friend back down. "Stay, stay, stay."

Irving was confused. He looked at Joe for answers, but Joe just smiled back.

"Well, I guess I'll just stay until Francesca gets here," said Irving.

"Yes, stay. The waiter will bring us our drinks soon," said Joe.

The waiter brought the drinks. Irving raised his glass.

"Cheers, Smithy," he said with a smile.

"Gosh, if your hair were just a little bit longer, you would look just like —"

Again, Joe kicked Irving under the table. This time, he kicked so hard that Irving fell out of his chair.

"Oh!" Ann cried out in shock.

"What are you doing, Joe?" yelled Irving.

Joe rushed to his friend and helped him up.

"It looks like you hurt yourself here," said Joe, looking at Irving's neck. "Here, let me help you get fixed up."

Joe held his friend firmly by the neck and led him away from the table. When they were far from Ann, Joe let go of Irving.

"What is going on?" asked Irving. He was angry and ready for some answers.

"Ok, Irving. What would you do for five thousand dollars?" Joe asked. Irving suddenly got quiet and serious.

## Chapter 4: The Three Friends

"Five thousand dollars?" Irving asked.

"Yes. She doesn't know that I'm a news reporter. This is the biggest story I've ever done, Irving! And I need pictures!" said Joe. Irving's eyes grew big.

"You mean that girl really is Princess Ann?" asked Irving.

"Yes. And if you work with me today, I'll give you twenty-five percent of the money," said Joe.

"It's a deal!" said Irving. The two men shook hands.

"Ok, now do you have your secret camera?" asked Joe.

"Of course I do," said Irving. He took a cigarette lighter out of his pocket. The lighter had a hidden camera in it.

"Well then, let's get to work!" said Joe. The two walked back to the table.

"Is your neck better now?" asked Ann.

"Yes, Joe helped me. I'm just fine," said Irving. Once everyone was sitting again, Irving took out his cigarettes from his pocket.

"Would you like a cigarette?" Irving asked Ann.

"Yes, thank you," said Ann. She took one and Irving lit it for her with his cigarette-lighter camera. He also took her picture without her noticing.

"I've never had a cigarette before!" said Ann.

"So, what shall we do today?" asked Joe. "Shall we make a list of things to do?"

"Oh, no! No lists, please," said Ann. "Let's just go and see what happens."

The three friends agreed and got up to leave. Just then, Francesca entered Rocca's, looking for Irving.

"Oh, I'm sorry, honey," Irving said in a hurry. "I have to work now. I'll see you later!"

## Chapter 4: The Three Friends

Irving left the restaurant with Ann and Joe.

At the same time, the general, the countess, and the ambassador were across town at the airport. Many men in dark suits and hats were getting off of a special airplane. The ambassador looked very worried.

"I hope these men get the job done with as little trouble as possible," the ambassador said.

"They will find the princess," said the general. "Don't worry."

Chapter 5
# *Seeing Rome*

Across town, near the Coliseum, Joe drove his scooter. Ann rode on the back. Irving followed in his open-topped car. Ann smiled as she looked at the sights. They stopped to go inside the Coliseum for a tour. After that, the three were back on the road. While Joe and Ann rode the scooter, Irving took pictures of Ann. He almost lost control of his car several times.

At a busy intersection, a policeman stopped Joe and Ann. Joe got off of the

## Chapter 5: Seeing Rome

scooter to talk to the policeman. As he did so, Ann put her hands on the handlebars just to see how it felt. She pressed the wrong thing, and all of a sudden, the scooter was moving!

Ann cried out in shock.

"Oh no!" cried Joe. He excused himself from the policeman and ran after Ann. Irving started taking many pictures.

Ann drove the scooter onto the sidewalk and through a crowd of people. Joe ran after her, yelling at her to stop. But Ann was not afraid anymore. In fact, she was now laughing and enjoying herself!

Joe caught up to the scooter and jumped on.

"Let me take the controls," he said.

"No, I can do this!" Ann said, laughing. All Joe could do was laugh with her.

Ann drove the scooter this way and that. She turned a corner and almost crashed into a car. But Ann kept driving, causing traffic and people to get out of her way. She laughed the whole time. The police began to chase Ann and Joe. Some ran after them, some followed in cars. Ann kept driving for as long as she could, but the police finally

## Chapter 5: Seeing Rome

caught up to the scooter. Irving caught up to them as well.

The next thing they knew, Joe, Ann, and Irving were at the police station, facing a judge. The judge asked questions in Italian and Joe answered. Joe put his arm around Ann, and the judge smiled. The judge let the three go. As they walked out, Joe and Ann held hands. The people at the police station all smiled and waved at Joe and Ann as they left. Irving laughed the whole way.

"Joe! You're such a good liar," Irving said. "You and Ann were going to church on a scooter to get married? That's a good one!"

Irving could not stop laughing.

"I was a good liar too, wasn't I?" said Ann.

"The best I ever met," said Joe. "Hey, I have an idea. Come on, I want to show you something."

They walked to a dark stone building. On

one wall was a large face carved into the stone. The face had a dark hole for a mouth.

"This is the Mouth of Truth," Joe told Ann. "People say that if you're a liar and you put your hand in here, your hand will get bitten off."

"Oh, that's terrible!" said Ann.

"Let's see you do it," said Joe. Ann looked worried, but she put out her hand slowly. Irving took more pictures with his hidden camera as the princess's hand got closer and closer to the stone mouth. At the last minute, Ann dropped her hand. She was too afraid to go further.

"Let's see you do it," she said to Joe.

"Fine," said Joe. He raised his hand slowly to the stone mouth. Then, shaking a little bit,

## Chapter 5: Seeing Rome

he put his hand into the hole. At first, he put in just his fingers, then he put in his whole hand. Ann watched, standing still with fear.

All of a sudden, Joe gave a loud cry. He pulled at his hand, as if the mouth had it and wouldn't let go. Ann screamed and pulled him from behind. Joe finally got his arm out of the hole, but his hand was gone!

Ann screamed and covered her face with her hands. Smiling, Joe took his hand out of his coat sleeve. He had only been hiding it!

Ann gave a cry and rushed toward Joe. She began laughing and beating his chest.

"You liar! Oh, you're terrible! You never hurt your hand!" she said.

"I was only joking," said Joe, laughing. "I'm sorry. Are you ok?"

"Yes," said Ann, calming down.

Irving took photographs of the whole event.

"Come on," said Joe. "I have another place I want to take you."

The three drove in Irving's car and arrived on a quiet street. They got out of the car and walked to a wall that lined the street. The wall was covered from top to bottom with little hand-painted signs. An old woman was on her knees, praying in front of the wall. When she finished, she crossed herself and got up to go.

Ann walked up to the wall.

"What are all these little signs? What does the writing say?" she asked.

"Well, each one is about a wish that came true," said Joe. "It all started during the war. One day, airplanes dropped bombs right here, and a man and his children were caught on the street. They ran over to this wall for safety. Bombs fell very close but no one was hurt. Later on, the man came back

## Chapter 5: Seeing Rome

and put up the first of these little signs. Since then, the wall has become sort of a holy place. People come, and whenever their wishes come true, they put up a little sign."

"What a lovely story," said Ann.

"Read some of these," said Joe. "And make your own wish."

Ann lowered her head to make a wish. Irving acted like he was lighting another cigarette to take more pictures.

"What did you wish for?" asked Joe.

"I can't tell you, but the chances of my wish coming true are very small," said Ann with a little sadness.

"Well, what shall we do next?" asked Joe.

"I heard about a wonderful place for dancing on a boat," said Ann. Her voice was full of hope.

"Oh, you must mean the boats down on the river Saint Angelo," said Joe.

"Yes! That's it! Can we go?"

"Hey, why not?" said Irving.

"Anything you wish," said Joe. "And, um, I think Irving has to go now."

"I do?" asked Irving.

"Yes, you know, for that big business meeting tomorrow you have to get ready for," said Joe.

"Oh, right," said Irving, acting like he just remembered something important. "The big business meeting. Well, see you later, Smithy."

"Good luck on your business meeting," said Ann.

As Irving turned to go, Ann and Joe walked back toward the street. They saw a horse-drawn carriage. Joe asked Ann if she would like to ride in the carriage to the dance. She said yes and they got in.

CHAPTER 6
# *The Dance at the River*

At the river, Joe paid for Ann as she watched the nighttime scene around her. There was lively music, lights, and many people dancing on a boat. They walked onto the dance floor and started to dance.

Two men in black suits and hats stood to the side and watched the people dance. Suddenly, one of the men noticed Joe and Ann dancing. He stood on his toes to get a better look. The other man also noticed them. He said something to his partner, and then he ran down the steps, away from the dancers.

Ann and Joe continued to dance. The next song was slower, and they danced a little closer. Ann rested her head on Joe's shoulder. She smiled, her eyes closed.

When the song finished, the dancers clapped. Joe and Ann walked off the dance floor and sat down at a table.

"Joe Bradley," said Ann, "if you don't mind my saying, I think you are wonderful."

"Oh," said Joe, smiling, "thank you very much."

"You spent all day doing all the things I wanted to do," said Ann. "Why?"

Joe looked uneasy.

"Um, well, it seemed like the right thing to do," he said.

"That is so kind of you. I have never met anybody so kind," Ann said.

Joe looked down, trying to hide how bad

## Chapter 6: The Dance at the River

he felt about lying to Ann.

"It was no trouble," said Joe.

"You are completely unselfish," said Ann.

"Let's go have a drink at the bar," said Joe, changing the subject. Joe took her hand and they walked over.

At the bar, a man stopped Ann. It was the barber who cut her hair that afternoon.

"Ah! You decided to come!" said the barber. "I looked for you for a long time. I thought maybe you didn't come."

Ann laughed.

"Your hair—all gone!" said the barber.

"It's nice, isn't it?" said Ann.

"Very nice," said the barber.

Ann introduced Joe.

"This is Mr. Bradley," she told the barber.

"I am Mario Delani," said the barber.

"It's nice to meet you," said Joe. "Are you two old friends?"

"He cut my hair today," said Ann. "He invited me here tonight."

The band started playing again, and Mario asked Ann to dance. Ann took his hand and they went out onto the dance floor. Joe watched them dance for a moment, then took out a notebook to quickly write something down. Just then, Irving came on the boat and found Joe. He had his real camera with him this time.

"Did I miss anything?" Irving asked.

"No, friend, you are just in time," said Joe. He pointed at Ann dancing with Mario, and Irving smiled.

"Who is she dancing with?" Irving asked.

"A barber. He cut her hair this afternoon and made a date for tonight."

Ann and Mario kept dancing, having a great time.

"'The Princess and the Barber,'" Irving

## Chapter 6: The Dance at the River

joked. He put his camera on the table and Joe stood in front of it, hiding it from view. Irving watched Ann and waited. Then, at the right moment, he gestured to Joe. Joe jumped out of the way, and the camera flashed. Joe jumped back in front of the camera and took a drink from his glass, acting as if nothing happened. Irving did the same, but he got the picture he wanted.

Ann looked over at Joe. Seeing Irving too, she smiled and waved. Irving raised his glass to her.

At this time, Secret Service men came in several cars and gathered outside. Some walked over to the tables on either side of the dance floor. The song ended, and the dancers cheered for the musicians.

"Thank you for the dance," Mario said to Ann.

One of the Secret Service men walked

over to them. He told Mario something in Italian, and suddenly Mario looked afraid. He smiled at Ann, said goodbye, then walked away. The Secret Service man began to dance with Ann.

"Your Highness, you will dance quietly toward the door," the Secret Service man said into Ann's ear.

"No," she said, and she tried hard to pull away.

"Princess, please," said the Secret Service man. He pulled her to the side of the dance floor.

"You made a mistake," Ann said in Italian. She acted like she didn't speak English. "Please, let me go!"

When the Secret Service man did not let her go, Ann began to yell.

"Let me go!" she cried. "Mr. Bradley!"

Joe looked up from his drink, looking for

## Chapter 6: The Dance at the River

her in the crowd of dancers.

"Mr. Bradley!" she cried out again.

Joe and Irving saw Ann at the same time. She was still trying to pull away from the Secret Service man. Another Secret Service man came to her side and the two tried to pull her off of the boat toward the steps. Joe and Irving rushed to her side.

Joe hit one of the Secret Service men in the face and he pushed the other one away. Joe took Ann's arm and was pulling her away when another Secret Service man ran to stop them. Joe hit him in the face too, and Irving fought with another Secret Service man.

Joe and Ann ran to the other side of the dance floor, where dancers were standing and watching the action. Joe saw more Secret Service men coming from that side, so he ran back the other way with Ann. But he met another group of Secret Service men.

Having no other choice, Joe pushed Ann to the side and threw one of the men over the side of the boat. He fell into the water. Ann threw a lifejacket down to him. The crowd of dancers cheered.

Irving fought with another Secret Service man. He pulled Irving's beard, so Irving hit him hard in the face. Mario Delani watched the fight. He decided to join in to help Joe and Irving.

The leader of the band gestured for the band to start playing again. Lively music joined the fighting on the dance floor.

While Joe, Irving, and Mario fought the Secret Service men, two of the men caught Ann and began to pull her away. Joe ran after her, and Irving followed with his camera. Joe pushed one of the men to the ground. The other man let go of Ann to hit Joe. Ann ran away and picked up a guitar

## Chapter 6: The Dance at the River

lying near the band. She stood behind the Secret Service man on a chair. The drummer of the band played a drum roll as she lifted the guitar over her head. She brought it down hard on the Secret Service man's head. The man stood still for a moment, shocked.

Irving tried to get his camera ready and said to Ann, "Hit him again, Smithy!" The drummer played another drum roll and Ann brought the guitar over the man's head again. This time, the camera flashed and Irving took her picture.

People started to hear the sound of police cars. Soon policemen were on the dance floor. As they stopped the fight, Joe, Ann, and Irving left the boat.

As the three walked toward Irving's car, they saw more police coming toward them.

"Police!" said Joe to Irving. "We'll go

across the bridge, but you keep going this way."

Joe and Ann ran across a bridge while Irving walked up to the police. He talked to them, trying to take up all their attention. But two policemen saw Joe and Ann and ran after them.

As Joe and Ann walked along the other side of the river, a Secret Service man followed them. He surprised them from behind. He hit Joe in the face, and Joe fell into the river. Ann jumped into the river after him, just as the Secret Service man tried to catch her. Then, the two policemen who ran after them across the bridge arrested the Secret Service man.

Back at the dance, the police were arresting all the Secret Service men. They led one man away who still had his head through a guitar.

Chapter 7
## *Two Hearts*

Joe and Ann swam to a large rock and got out of the river. They sat down, wet and cold. Joe rubbed Ann's arms to try to keep her warm.

"Are you ok?" Joe asked.

"I'm fine, how are you?"

"Oh, just great!" said Joe. They both laughed.

"You know, you were great back there," he said.

"You weren't so bad either," said Ann. She

looked up into his eyes.

Joe leaned forward and kissed her. Then they looked into each other's eyes.

"Well, um...I guess we better get going," said Joe.

They stood up and hurried back to Joe's apartment.

Back at the apartment, Joe played the radio softly and poured two glasses of wine. In the bathroom Ann changed out of her wet clothes and into some of Joe's clothes. She fixed her hair. When she was done, she opened the door and joined Joe.

"Are your clothes all ruined?" asked Joe.

"No, they will be dry soon," said Ann, smiling.

"You look good," said Joe. "You should always wear my clothes."

"It seems that I always do," said Ann with a smile.

## Chapter 7: Two Hearts

"I thought a little wine would be good," said Joe, handing her a glass.

"Shall I cook something?" asked Ann. She drank her wine.

"You can't," said Joe. "I don't have a kitchen. I always eat out."

"Do you like that?"

"Well, life isn't always what one likes, is it?" said Joe.

"No, it isn't," said Ann sadly. She looked away and sat down.

"Are you tired?" asked Joe.

"A little."

"You have had quite a day."

"A wonderful day!" said Ann. She smiled as the radio announcer came on.

"This is the American Hour, from Rome," said the voice on the radio. "Now for news. Tonight there is no word from Princess Ann, who fell ill yesterday. She was on the last part of her European tour. This has made some think that her condition must be serious. Many in our country are worried for her health."

Ann stood up and turned off the radio.

"The news can wait until tomorrow," she said.

"Yes," said Joe.

"May I have a little more wine? I'm sorry I couldn't cook us some dinner."

"Did you learn how to cook in school?" asked Joe, pouring her more wine.

"Yes. I'm a very good cook. I can sew too, and clean a house, and iron. I learned to do all those things—"

Ann stopped suddenly, then continued.

"—But I haven't had the chance to do it for anyone," she finished. She turned away sadly.

"Well, then it looks like I will have to

## Chapter 7: Two Hearts

move out and get myself a place with a kitchen," said Joe.

"Yes," Ann said with a sad smile. The two looked at each other without saying another word for a few moments. Ann looked away and drank the rest of her wine quickly.

"I... I will have to go now," she said. There were tears in her eyes. Joe watched her as she stood still for a moment. Then she ran into his arms and started to cry on his shoulder.

"Anya, there is something I want to tell you," said Joe, holding her.

"No," said Ann. She kissed him. "Please, say nothing."

They held each other for a few more moments. Then Ann looked down and let go.

"I must get dressed," she said. Heartbroken, Joe watched her walk into the bathroom and shut the door.

Soon, they were driving through Rome without saying anything to each other.

"Stop at the next corner, please," said Ann, as they neared the embassy.

Joe slowed and stopped the car. He could see the embassy gate up ahead.

"I have to leave you now," said Ann without looking at him. "I'm going to that corner and turning. You must stay in the car and drive away. Promise not to watch me go beyond the corner. Just drive away and leave me, as I leave you."

"Yes," said Joe.

"I don't know how to say goodbye," said Ann. "I can't think of any words."

"Don't try," said Joe.

Again, Ann threw herself into his arms. She began to cry. Joe held her tightly and they kissed again. They held each other for a while, until Ann turned her head to look

## Chapter 7: Two Hearts

up the street. She looked at Joe again. They smiled weakly at each other. Then Ann turned away, opened the car door, and got out.

Without looking back, Ann walked quickly down the street. Her walk turned into a run. Joe watched after her until she turned around the corner. For a moment, Joe wanted to get out of the car and run after her. But instead, he turned on the car engine and drove away.

In the embassy, Princess Ann stood in a large room. She faced the ambassador, the general, and the countess. They were all dressed in their bed clothes. The countess was crying and wiping her nose.

"Your Royal Highness," said the ambassador, "you have spent twenty-four hours away. What happened during that time?"

"I was not feeling well," said Ann. "I am better now."

"Ma'am, you must appreciate that I have my duty, just as Your Highness has your duty," said the ambassador.

"Sir, you won't find it necessary to use that word with me again. If I did not completely understand my duty to my family and my country, I would not have come back tonight. Or, indeed, ever again," said Ann. "Now, I understand we have a very full day tomorrow. You must all get your rest. You may leave."

They stood still for a moment, then bowed and left. At the door, the countess picked up a tray. She brought it to the princess.

"No milk tonight," said Princess Ann. "Thank you, countess."

The countess bowed to the princess and

## Chapter 7: Two Hearts

left. She closed the door behind her.

Finally alone, Ann walked to the window. She sat down and looked at the city below for a long time.

CHAPTER *8*
# *The Last Meeting*

The next day, Joe sat in his window, looking out over the city. There was a knock at his door. Joe looked up with hope. He rushed to the door and opened it. But it was Mr. Hennessy. Joe turned away in disappointment.

"Well? Did you get it?" asked Mr. Hennessy wildly, walking into the room.

"Get what?" asked Joe.

"The Princess story—the special interview! Did you really get it?"

"No, no, I didn't get it," said Joe, turning

## Chapter 8: The Last Meeting

away.

"What? But that's impossible!" yelled Mr. Hennessy. "You're just keeping it from me!"

"What would I be keeping from you?" asked Joe.

"I've heard things, Joe. I know too much. First, you come into my office and ask me about a special interview. Next, you disappear. Then, a friend at the embassy tells me the princess isn't sick at all, but is having fun in the town!"

"What kind of newspaper man are you?" asked Joe. "You believe every little story that people tell you?"

"But that's not all," said Mr. Hennessy. "I heard about a fight down at a boat on the river. I heard eight Secret Service men were arrested. And suddenly, there's news that the princess is well again! Now, it all makes sense. You have that story. And don't think you can raise the price now, Joe. We had a deal! Now come on, where's that story?"

Mr. Hennessy pushed Joe aside and started looking through the papers on Joe's desk.

"I have no story," said Joe, pouring himself a glass of wine.

Just then, Irving burst through the door. He was carrying a large envelope.

"Joe! You've got to see these!" Irving said. He saw Mr. Hennessy.

"Oh you got here at the right time, Mr. Hennessy. Wait until you see these!" he said.

Joe threw his wine on Irving.

"What are you doing, Joe?" said Irving, shocked. "Look at my pants!"

"Yes, you better go in there and wash them off," said Joe, pointing to the bathroom.

As Irving walked toward the bathroom, he asked, "Did you tell Mr. Hennessy about Smithy?"

## Chapter 8: The Last Meeting

"Um," said Joe.

"Oh, Mr. Hennessy, wait until you hear about—" started Irving, but Joe tripped him. Irving fell to the floor.

"Joe!" yelled Irving.

"Ok, what kind of game are you two playing?" asked Mr. Hennessy. "Who's Smithy and what am I supposed to be looking at?"

Mr. Hennessy grabbed the envelope from Irving. Joe grabbed the envelope back.

"Oh, Smithy's just some person we met the other day. Not interesting at all. You wouldn't want to hear about him. And there is nothing in this envelope but a few pictures of some of Irving's models. Nothing to interest you," said Joe.

Irving, still on the floor, looked up in surprise at Joe.

"I don't care about all that," said Mr. Hennessy. "What I care about is this story you said you had when you came into my office yesterday."

"Yes, yesterday I thought I had a story. But I was wrong!" said Joe. "There is no story."

Irving got up and looked at Joe, confused.

"Fine," said Mr. Hennessy. He picked up his hat and got ready to go. "The princess is holding a press meeting today. Just go to that, will you? And you owe me five hundred dollars. A deal is a deal."

"Just take it out of my salary. Fifty dollars a week," said Joe.

Mr. Hennessy agreed and left. But now Irving wanted some answers.

"What is going on?" asked Irving. "Did we get a better deal from another newspaper?"

"Irving, I don't know how to tell you this, but..." Joe stopped for a moment to think. "But I don't want to write the story."

"You don't?"

## Chapter 8: The Last Meeting

"No. I can't do that to her," said Joe. "I don't want to do that to her." He looked down, heartbroken, and Irving suddenly understood.

"Oh, I see," said Irving, looking down also. "Well, do you at least want to see the pictures?"

Irving took the pictures out of the envelope. He spread them out on the bed. He grew excited as he showed them to Joe.

"Look at this one," said Irving, smiling.

Joe picked up a picture of Ann smoking her first cigarette. He laughed.

"That was at Rocca's," Joe said, remembering the moment.

"Or how about this one?" Joe said as he picked up another picture. "The Mouth of Truth."

"Or this one?" Irving picked up another. They both looked at it and laughed. It was of Ann dancing with Mario, the barber.

"I was thinking the title for this should be 'The Barber Cuts In,'" said Irving.

"Hey, that's good!" said Joe, laughing.

Irving handed Joe another one. It showed Ann hitting a Secret Service man over the head with a guitar.

"Wow!" said Joe. "What a picture!"

"How about this for a title: 'Body Guard Gets Body Blow'?"

Irving and Joe laughed long and hard together. But the laughter slowly went away. They were both quiet for a few moments. Irving looked at Joe and saw there was deep sadness in his eyes.

## Chapter 8: The Last Meeting

"Are you still going to the press meeting today?" asked Irving.

"Yes, I'll go," said Joe. "It's my job."

"I'll see you there," said Irving. He picked up his pictures and put them back in the envelope. He looked down at his wet pants again. He shook his head and walked out the door.

At the embassy, many reporters and photographers gathered in a large hall. Joe and Irving walked in and looked all around them. It was a beautiful room. At the front of the room was a rope that would separate the reporters from the princess. Beyond the rope was a stage and a few steps leading to a large, open door.

A royal official came into the room. He stood by the rope and began to speak loudly.

"Ladies and gentlemen," he said. "I am

honored to introduce to you Her Royal Highness, Princess Ann."

All the reporters moved closer to the rope and watched as Princess Ann entered the room. The ambassador, the general, the countess, and many others followed her. Joe and Irving stood at the front of the crowd and watched.

"Your Royal Highness," said the ambassador, "these are the people of the press."

Princess Ann stood on the stage and smiled at the crowd in greeting. As her eyes moved over the crowd, she saw Joe. A look of shock came over her and her smile went away. She looked away quickly and the ambassador gestured for her to sit and start the meeting.

"Ladies and gentlemen," said the royal official, "the princess will now answer your questions."

## Chapter 8: The Last Meeting

The chief of reporters was the first to speak.

"I would like to let you know, Your Highness, that we are all very pleased that you are no longer feeling ill," he said.

"Thank you," said Ann.

Another reporter spoke.

"Does Your Highness believe that the future of Europe will be helped by nations working together?" the reporter asked.

"I believe that nations working together will surely be helpful for the future of Europe," said Ann.

"What does Your Highness think of the Friendship Among Nations?" asked another reporter.

"I think highly of it," said Ann, "just as I think highly of the friendship among people." As she said this, she turned to look at Joe.

"I believe Your Highness will never have a reason to doubt friendship among people," said Joe, looking into her eyes.

## Chapter 8: The Last Meeting

"I am so glad to hear you say it," said Ann. The ambassador, the general, and the other officials standing around Ann looked at each other with worry. This was not in the planned answers the princess was supposed to give.

"Which of the cities visited did Your Royal Highness enjoy the most?" asked another reporter.

Ann looked at Joe.

"Each city in its own way..." said the general quietly, trying to remind Ann of what she was supposed to say.

"Each city in its own way was special," said Ann. "It would be difficult to choose—"

But then she suddenly stopped. She looked at Joe again and smiled.

"Rome," said Ann, smiling wide. "By all means, Rome. I will never forget my time here, for as long as I live."

"Even though you were ill, Your Highness?" asked another reporter.

"Even so," said Ann.

A royal official stepped forward to speak.

"Photographs may now be taken," he said.

Ann stood up, and the photographers all came toward her. Irving stepped forward and smiled at Ann as he took out his cigarette-lighter camera. He bent forward, looked into it, and pushed the button. Ann looked at Irving with shock. She realized he had been using it as a camera the whole time. Irving smiled at her. Ann looked at Joe, and he smiled back at her. Irving walked back to join Joe.

"Thank you, ladies and gentlemen," said the ambassador. Ann turned to him.

"I would now like to meet some of the ladies and gentlemen of the press," she said. The ambassador was surprised. This was not

## Chapter 8: The Last Meeting

in the plan either. But Ann walked down the steps, with the countess and general joining her. They removed the rope and Ann came toward the line of reporters and photographers.

"My name is Hitchcock, from the Chicago Daily News," said the first reporter.

"I'm so happy to see you, Mr. Hitchcock," said Ann, smiling and shaking his hand.

"Deutsche Presse Agend," said the next reporter, from Germany.

"Pleased to meet you," said Ann, shaking his hand.

Ann made her way down the line of reporters, greeting them all. She finally came to Irving.

"Irving Radovich, from C.R. Photo Service," said Irving.

"How do you do?" asked Ann, shaking his hand. Irving reached into his pocket and handed her an envelope.

"May I present Your Highness with some photos of your visit to Rome?" said Irving.

Ann took the envelope. She opened it and took out one of the pictures. It was the one of her hitting a Secret Service man with a guitar. She held back her laughter.

"Thank you so very much," she told Irving. Then she looked at Joe and walked toward him.

"Joe Bradley, from American News Service," said Joe. Ann shook his hand, trying to hold back her feelings.

"So happy, Mr. Bradley," she said. They smiled at each other, and she moved on.

"Stephen Hausen, from the London Telegraph," said the next reporter.

"Good afternoon," said Ann.

When Ann reached the last of the reporters in the front row, she turned and walked

## Chapter 8: The Last Meeting

back up the steps. The press applauded when she reached the top. Slowly, she turned to face them with a smile. Her eyes moved over the crowd and came to rest on Joe. He smiled back at her, and for a moment they just looked at each other. Then, Ann turned to go.

The princess walked slowly out of the room, followed by the ambassador, the general, the countess, and many other officers. The crowd of reporters also began to leave. Irving looked at Joe, but Joe just stood and looked at the empty stage. Irving looked down. Without saying a word, he also left. Soon, Joe was all alone, standing at the rope.

Joe put his hands in his pockets and turned around. Slowly, he walked away. At the door, he took one last look back, then walked out of the building.

# Word List

- 本文で使われている全ての語を掲載しています（LEVEL 1、2）。ただし、LEVEL 3 以上は、中学校レベルの語を含みません。
- 語形が規則変化する語の見出しは原形で示しています。不規則変化語は本文中で使われている形になっています。
- 一般的な意味を紹介していますので、一部の語で本文で実際に使われている品詞や意味と合っていないことがあります。
- 品詞は以下のように示しています。

|名 名詞|代 代名詞|形 形容詞|副 副詞|動 動詞|助 助動詞|
|---|---|---|---|---|---|
|前 前置詞|接 接続詞|間 間投詞|冠 冠詞|略 略語|俗 俗語|
|頭 接頭語|尾 接尾語|記 記号|関 関係代名詞| | |

---

## A

- □ **a** 冠 ①1つの, 1人の, ある ②〜につき
- □ **about** 副 ①およそ, 約 ②まわりに, あたりに be about to まさに〜しようとしている, 〜するところだ 前 ①〜について ②〜のまわりに[の]
- □ **across** 前 〜を渡って, 〜の向こう側に, (身体の一部に)かけて 副 渡って, 向こう側に
- □ **act** 動 演じる
- □ **action** 名 ①行動, 活動 ②動作, 行為
- □ **address** 名 住所, アドレス
- □ **afraid** 形 ①心配して ②恐れて, こわがって I'm afraid (that) 残念ながら〜, 悪いけれど〜
- □ **after** 前 ①〜の後に[で], 〜の次に ②《前後に名詞がきて》次々に〜, 何度も〜《反復・継続を表す》after that その後
- □ **afternoon** 名 午後
- □ **again** 副 再び, もう一度
- □ **against** 前 〜に対して, 〜にもたれて
- □ **agree** 動 同意する
- □ **agreement** 名 合意, 協定
- □ **ah** 間 《驚き・悲しみ・賞賛などを表して》ああ, やっぱり
- □ **ahead** 副 前方へ[に]
- □ **airplane** 名 飛行機
- □ **airport** 名 空港
- □ **all** 形 すべての, 〜中 all day 一日中, 明けても暮れても 代 全部, すべて(のもの[人]) not 〜 at all 少しも[全然]〜ない 名 全体 副 まったく, すっかり all of a sudden 突然, 前触れもなしに all over the news ニュースをにぎわせている all over the world 世界中に all the time いつも, その間ずっと by all means なんとしても, ぜひとも
- □ **all right** 形 大丈夫で, よろしい, 申し分ない, わかった, 承知した
- □ **allow** 動 ①許す, 《〜… to 〜》が〜するのを可能にする, …に〜させておく ②与える
- □ **almost** 副 ほとんど, もう少しで(〜するところ)
- □ **alone** 形 ただひとりの 副 ひとりで, 〜だけで
- □ **along** 前 〜に沿って 副 前へ, ずっと, 進んで
- □ **already** 副 すでに, もう
- □ **also** 副 〜も(また), 〜も同様に 接

# Word List

その上, さらに

- **always** 副 いつも, 常に not always 必ずしも～であるとは限らない
- **am** 動 ～である, (～に) いる[ある]《主語がIのときのbeの現在形》
- **ambassador** 名 大使
- **American** 形 アメリカ(人)の 名 アメリカ人
- **among** 前 (3つ以上のもの)の間で[に], ～の中で[に]
- **Amsterdam** 名 アムステルダム《オランダの首都》
- **an** 冠 ①1つの, 1人の, ある ②～につき
- **and** 接 ①そして, ～と… ②《同じ語を結んで》ますます ③《結果を表して》それで, だから
- **angry** 形 怒って, 腹を立てて
- **Ann** 名 アン《人名》Princess Ann アン王女
- **announcer** 名 アナウンサー
- **another** 形 ①もう1つ[1人]の ②別の 代 ①もう1つ[1人] ②別のもの
- **answer** 動 ①答える, 応じる ②《－ for ～》～の責任を負う 名 答え, 応答, 返事
- **any** 形 ①《疑問文で》何か, いくつかの ②《否定文で》何も, 少しも (～ない) ③《肯定文で》どの～も 代 ①《疑問文で》(～のうち) 何か, どれか, 誰か ②《否定文で》少しも, 何も [誰も] ～ない ③《肯定文で》どれも, 誰でも
- **Anya Smith** 名 アーニャ・スミス《人名》
- **anybody** 代 ①《疑問文・条件節で》誰か ②《否定文で》誰も (～ない) ③《肯定文で》誰でも
- **anymore** 副 《通例否定文, 疑問文で》今はもう, これ以上, これから
- **anyone** 代 ①《疑問文・条件節で》誰か ②《否定文で》誰も (～ない) ③《肯定文で》誰でも
- **anything** 代 ①《疑問文で》何か, どれでも ②《否定文で》何も, どれも (～ない) ③《肯定文で》何でも, どれでも 副 いくらか
- **anyway** 副 ①いずれにせよ, ともかく ②どんな方法でも
- **anywhere** 副 どこかへ[に], どこにも, どこへも, どこにでも
- **apartment** 名 アパート
- **applaud** 動 拍手かっさいする, 賞賛する
- **appreciate** 動 ①正しく評価する, よさがわかる ②価値[相場]が上がる ③ありがたく思う
- **are** 動 ～である, (～に) いる[ある]《主語がyou, we, theyまたは複数名詞のときのbeの現在形》
- **argue** 動 ①論じる, 議論する ②主張する
- **arm** 名 腕
- **around** 副 ①まわりに, あちこちに ②およそ, 約 前 ～のまわりに, ～のあちこちに
- **arrest** 動 逮捕する
- **arrive** 動 到着する, 到達する arrive at ～に着く
- **as** 接 ①《as ～ as …の形で》…と同じくらい～ ②～のとおりに, ～のように ③～しながら, ～しているときに ④～するにつれて, ～にしたがって ⑤～なので ⑥～だけれども ⑦～する限りでは 前 ①～として(の) ②～の時 as if あたかも～のように, まるで～みたいに as to ～に関しては, ～については, ～に応じて as well なお, その上, 同様に just as (ちょうど)であろうとおり so ～ as to … …するほど～で 副 同じくらい as ～ as one can できる限り～ as ～ as possible できるだけ～ as long as ～する以上は, ～である限りは as soon as ～するとすぐ, ～するや否や 代 ①～のような ②～だが
- **aside** 副 わきへ(に), 離れて

- **ask** 動 ①尋ねる, 聞く ②頼む, 求める  ask ~ if ~かどうか尋ねる
- **asleep** 形 眠って(いる状態の) 副 眠って, 休止して  fall asleep 眠り込む, 寝入る
- **at** 前 ①《場所・時》~に[で] ②《目標・方向》~に[を], ~に向かって ③《原因・理由》~を見て[聞いて・知って] ④~に従事して, ~の状態で
- **ate** 動 eat(食べる)の過去
- **Athens** 名 アテネ《ギリシャの首都》
- **attention** 名 注意, 集中
- **away** 副 離れて, 遠くに, 去って, わきに

## B

- **back** 名 ①背中 ②裏, 後ろ 副 ①戻って ②後ろへ[に]
- **bad** 形 悪い, へたな, まずい
- **balcony** 名 バルコニー
- **ball** 名 (大)舞踏会
- **band** 名 楽団, バンド
- **bar** 名 酒場, バー
- **barber** 名 理髪師, 床屋
- **bath** 名 入浴, 水浴, 風呂  take a bath 風呂に入る
- **bathroom** 名 ①浴室 ②手洗い, トイレ
- **be** 動 ~である, (~に)いる[ある], ~となる 助 ①《現在分詞とともに用いて》~している ②《過去分詞とともに用いて》~される, ~されている
- **beard** 名 あごひげ
- **beat** 動 打つ
- **beautiful** 形 美しい, すばらしい
- **because** 接 (なぜなら)~だから, ~という理由[原因]で
- **become** 動 ①(~)になる ②(~に)似合う ③becomeの過去分詞
- **bed** 名 ベッド, 寝所  get into bed ベッドに入る
- **been** 動 be(~である)の過去分詞 助 be(~している・~される)の過去分詞
- **before** 前 ~の前に[で], ~より以前に 接 ~する前に 副 以前に
- **began** 動 begin(始まる)の過去
- **behind** 前 ①~の後ろに, ~の背後に ②~に遅れて, ~に劣って 副 ①後ろに, 背後に ②遅れて, 劣って
- **believe** 動 信じる, 信じている, (~と)思う, 考える
- **below** 副 下に[へ]
- **bench** 名 ベンチ, 長いす
- **bent** 動 bend(曲がる)の過去, 過去分詞
- **best** 形 最もよい, 最大[多]の 名 《the -》最上のもの
- **bet** 動 賭ける
- **better** 形 ①よりよい ②(人が)回復して 副 ①よりよく, より上手に ②むしろ
- **between** 前 (2つのもの)の間に[で・の]
- **beyond** 前 ~を越えて, ~の向こうに
- **big** 形 ①大きい ②偉い, 重要な
- **bit** 名 《a -》少し, ちょっと  just a little bit ほんの少し
- **bite** 動 かむ, かじる  get bitten off かみちぎられる
- **bitten** 動 bite(かむ)の過去分詞
- **black** 形 黒い, 有色の
- **blanket** 名 毛布
- **blew** 動 blow(吹く)の過去
- **blow** 動 息を吹く  body blow 腹部へのパンチ  blow a kiss at ~にキスを送る 名 打撃
- **blue** 形 青い
- **boat** 名 ボート, 小舟, 船

## Word List

- **body** 名 体 body blow 腹部へのパンチ
- **body guard** 名 ボディーガード
- **bomb** 名 爆弾
- **Bonnachoven** 名 バンノックホーベン《人名》
- **borrow** 動 借りる, 借金する
- **boss** 名 上司
- **both** 代 両方, 両者, 双方
- **bottom** 名 底, 下部, 最下位
- **bought** 動 buy（買う）の過去, 過去分詞
- **bow** 動 (〜に) お辞儀する
- **box** 名 箱, 容器
- **Bradley** 名 ブラッドレイ《人名》
- **bread** 名 パン
- **bridge** 名 橋
- **bring** 動 持ってくる, 連れてくる bring down 打ち降ろす
- **brought** 動 bring（持ってくる）の過去, 過去分詞
- **build** 動 確立する
- **building** 名 建物, ビルディング
- **burst** 動 ①爆発する[させる] ②破裂する[させる] burst through 〜から突然現れる
- **business** 名 ①職業, 仕事 ②商売 business meeting 商談, 営業会議
- **busy** 形 ①忙しい ②にぎやかな, 交通が激しい
- **but** 接 ①でも, しかし ②〜を除いて **not 〜 but …** 〜ではなくて… 前 〜を除いて, 〜のほか は 副 ただ, のみ, ほんの
- **button** 名 ボタン, ボタン状の物
- **buy** 動 買う
- **by** 前 ①《位置》〜のそばに[で] ②《手段・方法・行為者・基準》〜によって, 〜で ③《期限》〜までには ④《通過・経由》〜を経由して, 〜を通って 副 そばに, 通り過ぎて
- **bye** 間 さようなら

## C

- **C.R. Photo Service** C・R・フォト・サービス《社名》
- **call** 動 ①呼ぶ, 叫ぶ ②電話をかける **call after** 後ろから呼び掛ける, 人を追いかけて呼ぶ, 呼び止める
- **calm** 動 静まる, 静める **calm down** 静まる
- **came** 動 come（来る）の過去
- **camera** 名 カメラ
- **can** 助 ①〜できる ②〜してもよい ③〜でありうる ④《否定文で》〜のはずがない **as 〜 as one can** できる限り〜 **Can you 〜?** 〜してくれますか。
- **cancel** 動 取り消す, 中止する
- **cannot** can（〜できる）の否定形（=can not）
- **car** 名 自動車 open-topped car オープンカー
- **card** 名 トランプ,《-s》トランプ遊び
- **care** 名 世話, 介護 **take care of** 〜の世話をする, 〜面倒を見る, 〜を管理する 動 ①《通例否定文・疑問文で》気にする, 心配する ②世話をする **care about** 〜を気に掛ける
- **carefully** 副 注意深く, 丹念に
- **carriage** 名 馬車 horse-drawn carriage 馬車
- **carry** 動 運ぶ, 連れていく, 持ち歩く
- **cart** 名 荷馬車, 荷車
- **carve** 動 彫る, 彫刻する
- **catch** 動 ①つかまえる ②追いつく ③（病気に）かかる **catch up to** 〜に追いつく
- **caught** 動 catch（つかまえる）の過去, 過去分詞

- **cause** 動(〜の)原因となる, 引き起こす
- **ch.** 略 chapter(章)の略
- **chair** 名 いす
- **champagne** 名 シャンパン
- **chance** 名 ①偶然, 運 ②好機 ③見込み
- **change** 動 ①変わる, 変える ②交換する
- **charge** 名 責任 in charge of 〜を任されて, 〜を担当して, 〜の責任を負って
- **chase** 動 ①追跡する, 追い[探し]求める ②追い立てる
- **cheer** 動 かっさいを送る
- **cheers** 間 乾杯
- **chest** 名 胸
- **Chicago Daily News** シカゴ・デイリー・ニュース《社名》
- **chief** 名 頭, 長
- **children** 名 child(子ども)の複数
- **choice** 名 選択
- **choose** 動 選ぶ, (〜に)決める
- **chose** 動 choose(選ぶ)の過去
- **church** 名 教会, 礼拝(堂)
- **cigarette** 名 (紙巻)たばこ
- **cigarette-lighter camera** シガレットライター型カメラ
- **city** 名 都市, 都会
- **clap** 動 (手を)たたく
- **clean** 動 掃除する, よごれを落とす
- **cleaning lady** 女性の清掃作業員
- **climb** 動 登る, 徐々に上がる climb into 〜に乗り込む
- **clock** 名 掛け[置き]時計
- **close** 形 ①近い ②親しい ③狭い closer and closer どんどん近づく 副 ①接近して ②密集して 動 ①閉まる, 閉める ②終える, 閉店する close 〜 behind …… を〜の後ろで閉める
- **closed** 動 close(閉まる)の過去, 過去分詞 形 閉じた, 閉鎖した
- **closet** 名 戸棚, 物置, 押し入れ
- **clothes** 名 衣服, 身につけるもの
- **coat** 名 コート
- **coffee** 名 コーヒー
- **cold** 形 寒い, 冷たい
- **Coliseum** 名 コロッセオ《古代ローマの円形闘技場》
- **come** 動 ①来る, 行く, 現れる ②(出来事が)起こる, 生じる ③〜になる ④comeの過去分詞 come along ①一緒に来る, ついて来る ②やって来る, 現れる ③うまくいく, よくなる, できあがる come back 戻る come in 中にはいる, やってくる, 出回る come into 〜に入ってくる come on いいかげんにしろ, もうよせ, さあ来なさい ②(人)に偶然出合う come out 出てくる, 出掛ける, 姿を現す, 発行される come out from 〜から出てくる come over やって来る, 〜の身にふりかかる come true 実現する come up 近づいてくる
- **completely** 副 完全に, すっかり
- **condition** 名 (健康)状態
- **confused** 形 困惑した, 混乱した
- **continue** 動 続く, 続ける, (中断後)再開する
- **control** 名 管理, 支配(力) lose control of 〜を制御できなくなる
- **cook** 動 料理する 名 料理人, コック
- **corner** 名 曲がり角, 角
- **couch** 名 長いす
- **could** 助 ①can(〜できる)の過去 ②《控え目な推量・可能性・願望などを表す》Could you 〜? 〜してくださいますか。
- **countess** 名 伯爵夫人
- **country** 名 国
- **couple** 名 一組, 男女のカップル
- **course** 名 of course もちろん, 当

# Word List

然
- □ **cover** 動 覆う, 包む, 隠す
- □ **crash** 動 (人・乗り物が)衝突する
- □ **cross** 動 横切る, 渡る
- □ **crowd** 名 群集, 雑踏, 多数, 聴衆
- □ **crown** 名 冠
- □ **cry** 動 泣く, 叫ぶ, 大声を出す, 嘆く **cry out** 叫ぶ **cut off** 切断する, 切り離す 名 泣き声, 叫び, かっさい
- □ **cup** 名 カップ, 茶わん
- □ **cut** 動 ①切る, 刈る ②短縮する, 削る ③cutの過去, 過去分詞 名 ①切ること, 切り傷 ②削除 ③ヘアスタイル

## D

- □ **daily** 形 毎日の, 日常の
- □ **dance** 動 踊る, ダンスをする 名 ダンス, ダンスパーティー
- □ **dancer** 名 踊り子, ダンサー
- □ **dark** 形 ①暗い, 闇の ②(色が)濃い, (髪が)黒い ③陰うつな
- □ **date** 名 デート **make a date** (時刻と場所を決めて)人と会う約束をする
- □ **day** 名 ①日中, 昼間 ②日, 期日 **all day** 一日中, 明けても暮れても **full day** 丸一日 **one day** (過去の)ある日, (未来の)いつか **the other day** 先日
- □ **dead** 形 死んでいる
- □ **deal** 名 取引 **a good [great] deal (of ~)** かなり[ずいぶん・大量] (の~), 多額(の~)
- □ **decide** 動 決定[決意]する, (~しようと)決める, 判決を下す **decide to do** ~することに決める
- □ **deep** 形 深い
- □ **delighted** 形 喜んでいる
- □ **desk** 名 机
- □ **Deutsche Presse Agend** ドイツ・プレス・アジェンダ《社名》
- □ **diamond** 名 ダイヤモンド
- □ **did** 動 do (~をする)の過去 助 doの過去
- □ **die** 動 死ぬ, 消滅する
- □ **different** 形 異なった, 違った, 別の, さまざまな
- □ **difficult** 形 困難な, むずかしい, 扱いにくい
- □ **dinner** 名 ディナー, 夕食
- □ **direction** 名 方向, 方角
- □ **disappear** 動 見えなくなる, 姿を消す, なくなる
- □ **disappointment** 名 失望
- □ **dizzy** 形 めまいがする, 目が回る, くらくらする
- □ **do** 助 ①《ほかの動詞とともに用いて現在形の否定文・疑問文をつくる》②《同じ動詞を繰り返す代わりに用いる》③《動詞を強調するのに用いる》動 ~をする
- □ **doctor** 名 医者
- □ **does** 動 do (~をする)の3人称単数現在 助 doの3人称単数現在
- □ **dollar** 名 ①ドル《米国などの通貨単位。記号 $》
- □ **done** 動 do (~をする)の過去分詞
- □ **door** 名 ドア, 戸 **walk out the door** ドアの外に出る, どこかに行く
- □ **doubt** 名 ①疑い, 不確かなこと ②未解決点, 困難 **no doubt** きっと, たぶん 動 疑う
- □ **down** 副 ①下へ, 降りて, 低くなって ②倒れて 前 ~の下方へ, ~を下って **down there** 下の方で[に]
- □ **downstairs** 副 階下で, 下の部屋で
- □ **drank** 動 drink (飲む)の過去
- □ **dream** 名 夢, 幻想 動 (~の)夢を見る, 夢想[想像]する
- □ **dress** 名 ドレス, 衣服, 正装 動 ①服を着る[着せる] ②飾る

- **drink** 動 飲む, 飲酒する 名 飲み物, 酒, 1杯
- **drive** 動 車で行く, (車を)運転する **drive away** 車で走り去る
- **driver** 名 運転手
- **drop** 動 下がる, 下げる
- **drove** 動 drive (車で行く)の過去
- **drum** 名 太鼓, ドラム **drum roll** ドラムの連打
- **drummer** 名 ドラム奏者, ドラマー
- **drunk** 形 (酒に)酔った, 酔いしれた
- **dry** 形 乾燥した
- **during** 前 〜の間(ずっと)
- **duty** 名 ①義務(感), 責任 ②職務, 任務

## E

- **each** 形 それぞれの, 各自の 代 それぞれ, 各自 副 それぞれに **each one** 各自 **each other** お互いに
- **ear** 名 耳
- **early** 形 (時間や時期が)早い
- **eat** 動 食べる, 食事する **eat out** 外食をする
- **eight** 名 8(の数字), 8人[個] 形 8の, 8人[個]の
- **either** 形 ①(2つのうち)どちらかの ②どちらでも **either side of** 〜の両側に **on either side** 両側に 副 ①どちらか ②《否定文で》〜もまた(…ない)
- **embassy** 名 大使館
- **empty** 形 空の, 空いている
- **end** 動 終わる, 終える
- **engine** 名 エンジン, 機関
- **English** 名 英語
- **enjoy** 動 楽しむ, 享受する **enjoy oneself** 楽しく過ごす, 楽しむ
- **enter** 動 入る
- **envelope** 名 封筒
- **especially** 副 特別に, とりわけ
- **Europe** 名 ヨーロッパ
- **European** 名 ヨーロッパ人 形 ヨーロッパ(人)の
- **even** 副 ①《強意》〜でさえも, 〜ですら, いっそう, なおさら ②平等に **even though** 〜であるけれども, 〜にもかかわらず
- **event** 名 出来事, 事件, イベント
- **ever** 副 ①今までに, これまで, かつて, いつまでも ②《強意》いったい
- **every** 形 ①どの〜も, すべての, あらゆる ②毎〜, 〜ごとの
- **everyone** 代 誰でも, 皆
- **everything** 代 すべてのこと[もの], 何でも, 何もかも
- **exactly** 副 ①正確に, 厳密に, ちょうど ②まったくそのとおり
- **excited** 形 興奮した, わくわくした
- **excitement** 名 興奮(すること)
- **excuse** 動 ①(〜の)言い訳をする ②許す, 容赦する, 免除する **excuse oneself** お先にと言って去る
- **explain** 動 説明する, 明らかにする, 釈明[弁明]する
- **eye** 名 目

## F

- **face** 名 顔, 顔つき **make a face** 顔をしかめる 動 直面する, 立ち向かう
- **fact** 名 事実, 真相 **in fact** つまり, 実は, 要するに
- **fall** 動 ①落ちる, 倒れる ②(ある状態に)急に陥る **fall asleep** 眠り込む, 寝入る **fall back** 後ろ向きに倒れる **fall ill** 病気になる **fall into** 〜に落ち込む **fall off** 落ちる, 落ち込む **fall out** 落ちる, 飛び出す

## Word List

- **family** 名 家族, 家庭, 一門, 家柄
- **famous** 形 有名な, 名高い
- **far** 副 ①遠くに, はるかに, 離れて ②《比較級を強めて》ずっと, はるかに **far from** ~から遠い, ~どころか
- **fear** 名 ①恐れ ②心配, 不安 **with fear** 怖がって
- **feel** 動 感じる, (~と)思う **feel like** ~がほしい, ~したい気がする, ~のような感じがする
- **feeling** 動 feel (感じる)の現在分詞 名 ①感じ, 気持ち ②触感, 知覚 ③同情, 思いやり, 感受性
- **feet** 名 foot (足)の複数
- **fell** 動 fall (落ちる)の過去
- **felt** 動 feel (感じる)の過去, 過去分詞
- **few** 形 ①ほとんどない, 少数の(~しかない) ②《a-》少数の, 少しはある
- **fifty** 名 50 (の数字), 50人[個] 形 50の, 50人[個]の
- **fight** 動 (~と)戦う, 争う **fight with** ~と戦う 名 ①戦い, 争い, けんか ②闘志, ファイト
- **fighting** 名 戦い, 戦闘
- **fill** 動 ①満ちる, 満たす ②《be-ed with ~》~でいっぱいである
- **finally** 副 最後に, ついに, 結局
- **find** 動 ①見つける ②(~と)わかる, 気づく, ~と考える ③得る **find one's way** たどり着く
- **fine** 形 ①元気な ②美しい, りっぱな, 申し分ない, 結構な
- **finger** 名 (手の)指
- **finish** 動 終わる, 終える **finish doing** ~するのを終える
- **firmly** 副 しっかりと, 断固として
- **first** 名 最初, 第一 (の人・物) **at first** 最初に, 初めのうちは 形 ①第一の, 最初の ②最も重要な **for the first time** 初めて 副 第一に, 最初に
- **five** 名 5 (の数字), 5人[個] 形 5の, 5人[個]の
- **fix** 動 ①固定する[させる] ②修理する ③決定する ④用意する, 整える **fix up** 回復させる, 身なりを整える
- **flash** 動 閃光を発する
- **floor** 名 床
- **follow** 動 ついていく, あとをたどる **followed by** その後に~が続いて
- **for** 前 ①《目的・原因・対象》~にとって, ~のために[の], ~に対して ②《期間》~間 ③《代理》~の代わりに ④《方向》~へ(向かって) 接 というわけは~, なぜなら~, だから
- **force** 動 強制する, 力ずくで~する, 余儀なく~させ
- **forget** 動 忘れる, 置き忘れる
- **forty** 名 40 (の数字), 40人[個] 形 40の, 40人[個]の
- **forward** 副 前方に
- **fought** 動 fight (戦う)の過去, 過去分詞
- **found** 動 find (見つける)の過去, 過去分詞
- **four** 名 4 (の数字), 4人[個] 形 4の, 4人[個]の
- **Francesca** 名 フランチェスカ《人名》
- **free** 形 自由な, 開放された, 自由に~でき
- **friend** 名 友だち, 仲間
- **friendship** 名 友人であること, 友情
- **from** 前 ①《出身・出発点・時間・順序・原料》~から ②《原因・理由》~がもとで
- **front** 名 正面, 前 **in front of** ~の前に, ~の正面に 形 正面の, 前面の
- **front-page** 形 (新聞などの)第1面の
- **fruit** 名 果物
- **full** 形 ①満ちた, いっぱいの, 満期

# ROMAN HOLIDAY

の ②完全な, 盛りの, 充実した **be full of** ～で一杯である **full day** 丸一日 名全部

- □ **fun** 名楽しみ, 冗談, おもしろいこと **have fun** 楽しむ
- □ **further** 副いっそう遠く, その上に, もっと
- □ **future** 名未来, 将来 形未来の, 将来の

## G

- □ **game** 名ゲーム, 試合, 遊び, 競技
- □ **garden** 名庭, 庭園
- □ **gate** 名①門, 扉, 入り口 ②(空港・駅などの)ゲート
- □ **gather** 動集まる, 集める
- □ **gave** 動 give (与える) の過去
- □ **general** 名大将, 将軍
- □ **gentlemen** 名 gentleman (紳士) の複数
- □ **Germany** 名ドイツ《国名》
- □ **gesture** 動身振り[手振り]で示す
- □ **get** 動①得る, 手に入れる ②(ある状態に)なる, いたる ③わかる, 理解する ④～させる, ～を(…の状態に)する ⑤(ある場所に)達する, 着く **get back** 戻る, 帰る **get bitten off** かみちぎられる **get going** ①急ぐ ②出かける, 出発する **get in** 中に入る, 乗り込む **get into** ～に入る, 入り込む **get into bed** ベッドに入る **get off** (～から)降りる **get out** ①外に出る, 出て行く, 逃げ出す ②取り出す, 抜き出す **get out of** ～から下車する, ～から取り出す, ～から外へ出る[抜け出る] **get ready** 用意[支度]をする **get to** (事)を始める, ～に達する[到着する] **get up** 起き上がる, 立ち上がる **get up to** ～しようと立ち上がる **I don't get it.** 分からない, 理解できない。
- □ **girl** 名女の子, 少女

- □ **give** 動①与える, 贈る ②伝える, 述べる ③(～を)する **give someone a shot** (人)に注射をする **give up** あきらめる, やめる, 引き渡す
- □ **glad** 形①うれしい, 喜ばしい ②《be‐to～》～してうれしい, 喜んで～する
- □ **glass** 名コップ, グラス
- □ **go** 動①行く, 出かける ②動く ③進む, 経過する, いたる ④(ある状態に)なる **be going to** ～するつもりである **get going** ①急ぐ ②出かける, 出発する **go across** 横断する, 渡る **go and** ～しに行く **go away** 立ち去る **go by** そばを通る **go home** 帰宅する **go in** 中に入る, 開始する **go into** ～に入る, (仕事)に就く **go on** 起こる, 発生する **go out** 外出する, 外へ出る **go with** ～と一緒に行く **got to** ～しなければならない **let go** 手を放す, 行かせる **let go of** ～から手を離す **ready to go** すっかり準備が整った
- □ **gone** 動 go (行く) の過去分詞 形去った
- □ **good** 形①よい, 上手な, 優れた, 美しい ②(数量・程度が)かなりの, 相当な 間よかった, わかった, よろしい 名①善, 徳, 益, 幸福 ②《-s》財産, 品, 物質
- □ **goodbye** 間さようなら 名別れのあいさつ
- □ **gosh** 間おやっ!, えっ!
- □ **got** 動 get (得る) の過去, 過去分詞 **got to** ～しなければならない
- □ **grab** 動①ふいにつかむ, ひったくる ②横取りする
- □ **great** 形①大きい, 広大な, (量や程度が)たいへんな ②偉大な, 優れた ③すばらしい, おもしろい
- □ **greet** 動①あいさつする ②(喜んで)迎える
- □ **greeting** 動 greet (あいさつする) の現在分詞 名あいさつ(の言葉), あ

# Word List

いさつ（状）

- **grew** 動 grow（成長する）の過去
- **ground** 名 地面, 土, 土地
- **group** 名 集団, 群
- **guard** 名 ①警戒, 見張り ②番人 **body guard** ボディーガード
- **guess** 動 ①推測する, 言い当てる ②（～と）思う
- **guest** 名 客, ゲスト
- **guitar** 名 ギター

## H

- **had** 動 have（持つ）の過去, 過去分詞 助 have の過去《過去完了の文をつくる》
- **hair** 名 髪, 毛
- **half** 名 半分 形 半分の, 不完全な 副 半分, なかば, 不十分に
- **hall** 名 公会堂, ホール, 大広間, 玄関
- **hand** 名 手
- **hand-painted** 形 手描きの, 手塗りの
- **handlebars** 名 ハンドルバー
- **happen** 動 ①（出来事が）起こる, 生じる ②偶然［たまたま］～する
- **happy** 形 幸せな, うれしい, 幸運な, 満足して
- **hard** 形 ①堅い ②激しい, むずかしい ③熱心な, 勤勉な ④無情な, 耐えがたい, 厳しい, きつい 副 ①一生懸命に ②激しく ③堅く
- **has** 動 have（持つ）の3人称単数現在 助 have の3人称単数現在《現在完了の文をつくる》
- **hat** 名 （縁のある）帽子
- **hate** 動 嫌う, 憎む,（～するのを）いやがる
- **have** 動 ①持つ, 持っている, 抱く ②（～が）ある, いる ③食べる, 飲む ④経験する,（病気に）かかる ⑤催す,

開く ⑥（人に）～させる **have to** ～しなければならない **don't have to** ～する必要はない **have fun** 楽しむ 助《〈have＋過去分詞〉の形で現在完了の文をつくる》～した, ～したことがある, ずっと～している

- **he** 代 彼は［が］
- **head** 名 頭
- **health** 名 健康（状態）
- **hear** 動 聞く, 聞こえる **hear about** ～について聞く
- **heard** 動 hear（聞く）の過去, 過去分詞
- **heart** 名 ①心臓, 胸 ②心, 感情, ハート ③中心, 本質
- **heartbroken** 形 悲しみに打ちひしがれた
- **held** 動 hold（つかむ）の過去, 過去分詞
- **hello** 間 こんにちは, やあ
- **help** 動 ①助ける, 手伝う **help someone up** ひとを助け起こす, ささえる
- **helpful** 形 役に立つ, 参考になる
- **Hennessy** 名 ヘネシー《人名》
- **her** 代 ①彼女を［に］ ②彼女の
- **here** 副 ①ここに［で］ ②《- is ［are］～》ここに～がある ③さあ, そら **here are** ～ こちらは～です。 **Look here.** ほら。ねえ。 名 ここ
- **herself** 代 彼女自身
- **hey** 間 ①《呼びかけ・注意を促して》おい, ちょっと ②へえ, おや, まあ
- **hid** 動 hide（隠れる）の過去, 過去分詞
- **hidden** 形 隠れた, 秘密の
- **hide** 動 隠れる, 隠す, 隠れて見えない, 秘密にする
- **highly** 副 ①大いに, 非常に ②高度に, 高位に ③高く評価して, 高価で **think highly of** ～を高く評価する, 尊敬する

# ROMAN HOLIDAY

- **highness** 名《H-》殿下 Your (Royal) Highness《呼びかけ》殿下
- **him** 代 彼を[に]
- **himself** 代 彼自身
- **his** 代 ①彼の ②彼のもの
- **hit** 動 打つ, なぐる
- **Hitchcock** 名 ヒッチコック《人名》
- **hmm** 間 ふむ, ううむ《熟考・疑問・ためらいなどを表す》
- **hold** 動 ①つかむ, 持つ, 抱く ②保つ, 持ちこたえる ③収納できる, 入れることができる ④(会などを)開く **hold back** (事実・本心などを)隠す, (感情を)抑える, 自制する **hold out** ①差し出す, (腕を)伸ばす ②持ちこたえる, 粘る, 耐える
- **hole** 名 穴
- **holiday** 名 祝祭日, 休暇
- **holy** 形 聖なる, 神聖な
- **home** 名 ①家, 自国, 故郷, 家庭 ②収容所 副 家に, 自国へ **go home** 帰宅する **take someone home** (人)を家まで送る
- **honey** 名《呼びかけ》かわいい人
- **honor** 名 ①名誉, 光栄, 信用 ②節操, 自尊心 動 尊敬する, 栄誉を与える
- **hope** 動 望む, (〜であるようにと)思う
- **horse-drawn** 形 馬に引かせた **horse-drawn carriage** 馬車
- **hour** 名 1時間, 時間
- **house** 名 家, 家庭
- **how** 副 ①どうやって, どれくらい, どんなふうに ②なんて (〜だろう) ③《関係副詞》〜する方法 **How about 〜?** 〜はどうですか。〜しませんか。 **how to** 〜する方法
- **hundred** 名 ①100 (の数字), 100人 [個] ②《-s》何百, 多数 形 ①100の, 100人 [個] の ②多数の
- **hurry** 動 急ぐ, 急がせる, あわてる 名 急ぐこと, 急な必要 **in a hurry** 急いで, あわてて
- **hurt** 動 傷つける, 痛む, 害する 名 傷, けが, 苦痛, 害

# I

- **I** 代 私は[が]
- **ice cream** アイスクリーム
- **idea** 名 考え, 意見, アイデア, 計画
- **if** 接 もし〜ならば, たとえ〜でも, 〜かどうか **as if** あたかも〜のように, まるで〜みたいな **ask 〜 if** 〜かどうか尋ねる
- **ill** 形 病気の, 不健康な **fall ill** 病気になる
- **important** 形 重要な, 大切な, 有力な
- **impossible** 形 不可能な, できない, あり [起こり] えない
- **in** 前 ①《場所・位置・所属》〜(の中)に[で・の] ②《時》〜(の時)に[の・で], 〜後(に), 〜の間(に) ③《方法・手段》〜で ④〜を身につけて, 〜を着て ⑤〜に関して, 〜について ⑥《状態》〜の状態で 副 中へ[に], 内へ[に]
- **inch** 名 ①インチ《長さの単位。1/12フィート, 2.54cm》 **every inch of** 〜のどこもかしこも
- **indeed** 副 ①実際, 本当に ②《強意》まったく
- **inside** 名 内部, 内側 形 内部 [内側] にある 副 内部 [内側] に 前 〜の内部 [内側] に
- **instead** 副 その代わりに
- **interest** 動 興味を起こさせる
- **interesting** 形 おもしろい, 興味を起こさせる
- **intersection** 名 交差点
- **interview** 名 会見, 面接
- **into** 前 ①《動作・運動の方向》〜の中へ[に] ②《変化》〜に[へ]
- **introduce** 動 紹介する, 採り入れ

## WORD LIST

- **invitation** 名招待(状), 案内(状)
- **invite** 動①招待する, 招く ②勧める, 誘う ③〜をもたらす
- **iron** 動アイロンをかける
- **Irv** 名アーブ《人名, アービングの愛称》
- **Irving Radovich** アービング・ラドビッチ《人名》
- **is** 動 be (〜である)の3人称単数現在
- **it** 代①それは[が], それを[に] ②《天候・日時・距離・寒暖などを示す》 **I don't get it** 分からない, 理解できない。 **keep it from + 人** (人)に内緒にする **That's it.** それだけのことだ。
- **Italian** 形イタリア(人・語)の 名①イタリア人 ②イタリア語
- **its** 代それの, あれの

### J

- **job** 名仕事, 職, 雇用
- **Joe Bradley** ジョー・ブラッドレイ《人名》
- **join** 動一緒になる, 参加する **join in** 加わる, 参加する
- **joke** 名冗談, ジョーク 動冗談を言う, ふざける, からかう
- **judge** 名裁判官, 判事
- **jump** 動①跳ぶ, 跳躍する, 飛び越える, 飛びかかる ②(〜を)熱心にやり始める **jump into** 〜に飛び込む **jump on** 〜に飛びかかる **jump out** 飛び出る **jump out of** 〜から飛び出す
- **just** 副①まさに, ちょうど, (〜した)ばかり ②ほんの, 単に, ただ〜だけ ③ちょっと **just a little bit** ほんの少し **Just a minute.** ちょっと待って。 **just as** (ちょうど)であろうとおり **just in time** いよいよというときに, すんでのところで, やっと間に合って **just then** そのとたんに

### K

- **keep** 動①とっておく, 保つ, 続ける ②(〜を…に)しておく **keep it from + 人** (人)に内緒にする **keep on 〜[〜ing]** 〜し続ける, 繰り返し〜する
- **kept** 動 keep (とっておく)の過去, 過去分詞
- **key** 名かぎ, 手がかり
- **kick** 動ける, キックする
- **kind** 形親切な, 優しい 名種類 **kind of** ある程度, いくらか, 〜のような物[人]
- **king** 名王, 国王
- **kiss** 名キス **blow a kiss at** 〜にキスを送る 動キスする
- **kitchen** 名台所, 調理場
- **knee** 名ひざ
- **knew** 動 know (知っている)の過去
- **knock** 名戸をたたくこと[音]
- **know** 動①知っている, 知る, (〜が)わかる, 理解している ②知り合いである **you know** ご存知のとおり, そうでしょう

### L

- **lady** 名婦人, 夫人, 淑女, 奥さん **cleaning lady** 女性の清掃作業員
- **large** 形①大きい, 広い ②大勢の, 多量の
- **last** 形①《the -》最後の ②この前の, 先〜 ③最新の 名《the -》最後(のもの), 終わり
- **late** 形遅い 副遅れて, 遅く
- **later** 形もっと遅い, もっと後の

- 副後で, 後ほど **later on** もっと後で, のちほど
- **laugh** 動笑う 名笑い(声)
- **laughter** 名笑い(声)
- **lead** 動導く, 案内する **lead to ~** に至る, ~に通じる, ~を引き起こす
- **leader** 名指導者, リーダー
- **lean** 動①もたれる, 寄りかかる ②傾く, 傾ける
- **learn** 動学ぶ, 習う, 教わる, 知識[経験]を得る
- **least** 名最小, 最少 **at least** 少なくとも
- **leave** 動①出発する, 去る ②残す, 置き忘れる ③(~を…の)ままにしておく ④ゆだねる **leave for ~** に向かって出発する
- **led** 動 lead (導く)の過去, 過去分詞
- **left** 動 leave (去る, ~をあとに残す)の過去, 過去分詞
- **let** 動(人に~)させる, (~するのを)許す, (~をある状態に)する **let go** 手を放す, 行かせる **let go of ~** から手を離す
- **liar** 名うそつき
- **lie** 動①うそをつく ②横たわる, 寝る
- **life** 名生活, 暮らし, 世の中
- **lifejacket** 名ライフジャケット, 救命胴衣
- **lift** 動持ち上げる, 上がる
- **light** 名光, 明かり 動火をつける, 照らす, 明るくする
- **lighter** 名点火用具, ライター
- **like** 動好む, 好きである **would like to ~** したいと思う **Would you like ~?** ~はいかがですか。 前に似ている, ~のような **feel like ~** がほしい, ~したい気がする, ~のような感じがする **like this** このような, こんなふうに **look like ~** のように見える, ~に似ている **sound like ~** のように聞こえる 形似ている, ~のような 接あたかも~のように 名①好きなもの ②《the [one's] -》同じようなもの[人]
- **line** 名列 動整列する
- **liquor** 名(強い)酒, 蒸留酒
- **lira** 名リラ《イタリアの通貨単位, 2002年まで使用された》
- **list** 名名簿, 目録, 一覧表 動名簿[目録]に記入する
- **listen** 動《- to ~》~を聞く, ~に耳を傾ける
- **lit** 動 light (火をつける)の過去, 過去分詞
- **little** 形①小さい, 幼い ②少しの, 短い ③ほとんど~ない, 《a-》少しはある **just a little bit** ほんの少し 名少し(しか), 少量 副全然~ない, 《a-》少しはある
- **live** 動住む, 暮らす, 生きている
- **lively** 形元気のよい, 活発な
- **London** 名ロンドン《英国の首都》
- **London Telegraph** ロンドン・テレグラフ《社名》
- **long** 形①長い, 長期の ②《長さ・距離・時間などを示す語句を伴って》~の長さ[距離・時間]の 副長い間, ずっと **as long as** ~する以上は, ~である限りは **no longer** もはや~でない[~しない]
- **look** 動①見る ②(~に)見える, (~の)顔つきをする ③注意する ④《間投詞のように》ほら, ねえ **look away** 横を向く **look down** 見下ろす **look down at** ~に目[視線]を落とす **look for** ~を探す **Look here.** ほら。ねえ。 **look in** 中を見る, 立ち寄る **look into** ①~を検討する, ~を研究する ②~の中を見る, ~をのぞき込む **look like** ~のように見える, ~に似ている **look out** ①外を見る ②気をつける, 注意する **look out over** ~をはるかに見渡す **look over** ~越しに見る, ~を見渡す **look over at** ~の方を見る **look through** ~をのぞき込む **look up** 見上げる, 調べ

## Word List

る 名①一見, 目つき ②外観, 外見, 様子
- **lose** 動①失う, 迷う, 忘れる ②負ける, 失敗する
- **lost** 動 lose（失う）の過去, 過去分詞
- **lot** 名たくさん, たいへん,《a – of ~ / -s of ~》たくさんの~
- **loud** 形大声の, 騒がしい
- **loudly** 副大声で, 騒がしく
- **love** 名愛, 愛情, 思いやり
- **lovely** 形愛らしい, 美しい, すばらしい
- **lower** 動下げる, 低くする
- **luck** 名運, 幸運, めぐり合わせ
- **lying** 動 lie（横たわる）の現在分詞

## M

- **ma'am** 名奥さん, お嬢さん
- **made** 動 make（作る）の過去, 過去分詞
- **make** 動①作る, 得る ②行う,（~に）なる ③（~を…に）する,（~を…）させる **make a date**（時と場所を決めて）人と会う約束をする **make a face** 顔をしかめる **make a mistake** 間違いをする **make one's way** 進む, 行く, 成功する **make sense** 意味をなす, よくわかる **make sure** 確かめる, 確認する
- **man** 名男性, 人, 人類
- **many** 形多数の, たくさんの **so many** 非常に多くの
- **Mario Delani** マリオ・デラニ《人名》
- **marry** 動結婚する
- **may** 動①~かもしれない ②~してもよい, ~できる **May I ~?** ~してもよいですか。
- **maybe** 副たぶん, おそらく

- **me** 代私を［に］
- **mean** 動①意味する ②（~のつもりで）言う, 意図する ③~するつもりである 形①卑怯な, けちな, 意地悪な ②中間の
- **means** 名①手段, 方法 ②資力, 財産 ③mean（中間）の複数 **by all means** なんとしても, ぜひとも
- **meant** 動 mean（意味する）の過去, 過去分詞
- **medicine** 名薬
- **meet** 動①会う, 知り合いになる ②合流する, 交わる ③（条件などに）達する, 合う **meet with** ~に出会う **Nice to meet you.** お会いできてうれしい。
- **meeting** 動 meet（会う）の現在分詞 名集まり, ミーティング **business meeting** 商談, 営業会議
- **men** 名 man（男性）の複数
- **met** 動 meet（会う）の過去, 過去分詞
- **middle** 名中間, 最中 **in the middle of** ~の真ん中［中ほど］に
- **milk** 名牛乳, ミルク
- **mind** 名①心, 精神, 考え ②知性 動①気にする, いやがる ②気をつける, 用心する
- **minister** 名大臣, 閣僚, 公使
- **minute** 名①（時間の）分 ②ちょっとの間 **Just a minute.** ちょっと待って。
- **miss** 動~を見逃す
- **missing** 形欠けている, 行方不明の
- **mistake** 名誤り, 誤解, 間違い **make a mistake** 間違いをする
- **mmm** 間うーん
- **mmmm** 間うーん
- **model** 名モデル
- **moment** 名①瞬間, ちょっとの間 ②（特定の）時, 時期 **for a moment** 少しの間

## ROMAN HOLIDAY

- **money** 名 金, 通貨
- **moonlight** 名 月明かり, 月光
- **more** 形 ①もっと多くの ②それ以上の, 余分の 副 もっと, さらに多く, いっそう
- **morning** 名 朝, 午前
- **most** 副 最も(多く)
- **mouth** 名 ①口 ②言葉, 発言
- **Mouth of Truth** 名 真実の口《ローマの大きな人面の口》
- **move** 動 ①動く, 動かす ②感動させる ③引っ越す, 移動する move on 先に進む
- **Mr.** 名《男性に対して》~さん, ~氏, ~先生
- **much** 形(量・程度が)多くの, 多量の 副 ①とても, たいへん ②《比較級・最上級を修飾して》ずっと, はるかに too much 過度の
- **music** 名 音楽, 楽曲
- **musician** 名 音楽家
- **must** 助 ①~しなければならない ②~に違いない
- **my** 代 私の
- **myself** 代 私自身

## N

- **name** 名 名前
- **nation** 名 国, 国家
- **near** 前 ~の近くに, ~のそばに 動 近づく, 近寄る
- **necessary** 形 必要な, 必然の 名《-s》必要品, 必需品
- **neck** 名 首
- **need** 動 (~を)必要とする, 必要である need to do ~する必要がある
- **never** 副 決して[少しも]~ない, 一度も[二度と]~ない
- **new** 形 ①新しい, 新規の ②新鮮な, できたての

- **New York** ニューヨーク《米国の都市;州》
- **news** 名 報道, ニュース, 便り, 知らせ all over the news ニュースをにぎわせている
- **newspaper** 名 新聞(紙)
- **next** 形 ①次の, 翌~ ②隣の next to ~のとなりに, ~の次に 副 ①次に ②隣に
- **nice** 形 すてきな, よい, きれいな, 親切な Nice to meet you. お会いできてうれしい
- **night** 名 夜, 晩
- **nightgown** 名 ナイトガウン
- **nighttime** 名 夜間
- **nine** 名 9(の数字), 9人[個] 形 9の, 9人[個]の
- **no** 副 ①いいえ, いや ②少しも~ない 形 ~がない, 少しも~ない, ~どころでない, ~禁止 no doubt きっと, たぶん no longer もはや~でない[~しない] no use 役に立たない, 用をなさない
- **no one** 代 誰も[一人も]~ない
- **noon** 名 正午, 真昼
- **nose** 名 鼻, 嗅覚, におい
- **not** 副 ~でない, ~しない not ~ at all 少しも[全然]~ない not ~ but … ~ではなくて… not always 必ずしも~であるとは限らない not quite まったく~だというわけではない
- **notebook** 名 ノート, 手帳
- **nothing** 代 何も~ない[しない]
- **notice** 動 気づく, 認める
- **now** 副 ①今(では), 現在 ②今すぐに ③では, さて right now 今すぐに, たった今 形 今の, 現在の

## O

- **o'clock** 副 ~時

# Word List

- **of** 前 ①《所有・所属・部分》〜の,〜に属する ②《性質・特徴・材料》〜の,〜製の ③《部分》〜のうち ④《分離・除去》〜から

- **off** 副 ①離れて ②はずれて ③止まって ④休んで **take off**(衣服を)脱ぐ 前 〜を離れて,〜をはずれて,(値段が)〜引きの

- **office** 名 会社,事務所,職場

- **officer** 名 役人

- **official** 名 公務員,役人,職員 **royal official** 王室関係者

- **oh** 間 ああ,おや,まあ

- **ok** 形《許可・同意・満足などを表して》よろしい,正しい 間 それでは,さて

- **old** 形 ①年取った,老いた ②〜歳の ③古い,昔の

- **on** 前 ①《場所・接触》〜(の上)に ②《日・時》〜に,〜と同時に,〜のすぐ後で ③《関係・従事》〜に関して,〜について,〜して 副 身につけて,上に ②前へ,続けて

- **once** 接 〜するや否や

- **one** 名 1(の数字),1人[個] 形 ① 1の,1人[個]の ②ある〜 ③《the –》唯一の **one day**(過去の)ある日,(未来の)いつか 代 ①(一般の)人,ある物 ②一方,片方 ③〜なもの **each one** 各自 **one of** 〜の1つ[人] **this one** これ,こちら

- **one-way** 形 片道の,一方通行の,一方的な

- **oneself** 熟 **enjoy oneself** 楽しく過ごす,楽しむ **excuse oneself** お先にと言って去る **for oneself** 自分のために

- **only** 副 ①単に,〜にすぎない,ただ〜だけ ②やっと

- **onto** 前 〜の上へ[に]

- **open** 形 ①開いた,広々とした ②公開された 動 ①開く,始まる ②広がる,広げる ③打ち明ける

- **open-topped car** オープンカー

- **or** 接 ①〜か…,または ②さもないと ③すなわち,言い換えると

- **order** 動(〜するよう)命じる,注文する

- **other** 形 ①ほかの,異なった ②(2つのうち)もう一方の,(3つ以上のうち)残りの **each other** お互いに **the other day** 先日 代 ①ほかの人[物] ②《the –》残りの1つ 副 そうでなく,別に

- **our** 代 私たちの

- **out** 副 ①外へ[に],不在で,離れて ②世に出て ③消えて ④すっかり 形 ①外の,遠く離れた,②公表された 前 〜から外へ[に] 動 ①追い出す ②露見する ③(スポーツで)アウトにする

- **outside** 名 外部,外側 形 外部の,外側の 副 外へ,外側に 前 〜の外に[で・の・へ],〜の範囲を越えて

- **over** 前 ①〜の上の[に],〜を一面に覆って ②〜を越えて,〜以上に,〜よりまさって ③〜の向こう側の[に] ④〜の間 **all over the news** ニュースをにぎわせている **all over the world** 世界中に 副 上に,一面に,ずっと 形 ①上部の,上位の,過多の ②終わって,すんで

- **ow** 間 痛い!,あいた!

- **owe** 動(金を)借りている,(人に対して〜の)義務がある

- **own** 形 自身の

## P

- **pack** 動 荷造りする,詰め込む **pack up** 荷物をまとめる

- **paid** 動 **pay**(払う)の過去,過去分詞

- **pair** 名(2つから成る)一対,一組,ペア

- **pajamas** 名 パジャマ

- **pants** 名 ズボン,スラックス

## Roman Holiday

- **paper** 名 新聞
- **Paris** 名 パリ《フランスの首都》
- **park** 名 公園, 広場 動 駐車する
- **part** 名 部分, 割合
- **partner** 名 仲間, 同僚
- **party** 名 パーティー, 会, 集まり
- **pass** 動 過ぎる, 通る
- **past** 前 《時間・場所》~を過ぎて, ~を越して
- **pay** 動 ①支払う, 払う, 報いる, 償う ②割に合う, ペイする **pay back** 返済する, お返しをする
- **people** 名 ①(一般に)人々 ②民衆, 世界の人々, 国民, 民族 ③人間
- **percent** 名 パーセント, 百分率
- **perfectly** 副 完全に, 申し分なく
- **person** 名 ①人 ②人格, 人柄
- **phone** 名 電話
- **photo** 名 写真
- **photograph** 名 写真 動 写真を撮る
- **photographer** 名 写真家, カメラマン
- **pick** 動 ①(花・果実などを)摘む, もぐ ②選ぶ, 精選する ③つつく, つついて穴をあける, ほじくり出す ④(~を)摘み取る **pick up** 拾い上げる, 車で迎えに行く
- **picture** 名 ①絵, 写真, 《-s》映画 ②イメージ, 事態, 状況, 全体像 **take a picture** 写真を撮る
- **piece** 名 一片, 部分 **a piece of** 一切れの~
- **place** 名 ①場所, 建物 ②余地, 空間 ③《one's -》家, 部屋 動 置く, 配置する
- **plan** 名 計画, 設計(図), 案
- **planned** 形 計画された
- **play** 動 ①遊ぶ, 競技する ②(楽器を)演奏する
- **player** 名 競技者, 選手, 演奏者, 俳優
- **please** 動 喜ばす, 満足させる 間 どうぞ, お願いします
- **pleased** 形 喜んだ, 気に入った
- **pocket** 名 ポケット
- **point** 動 ①(~を)指す, 向ける ②とがらせる
- **police** 名 ①《the -》警察, 警官 ②公安, 治安
- **policeman** 名 警察官
- **policemen** 名 policeman(警察官)の複数
- **polite** 形 ていねいな, 礼儀正しい, 洗練された
- **possible** 形 ①可能な ②ありうる, 起こりうる **as ~ as possible** できるだけ~
- **pour** 動 ①注ぐ, 浴びせる ②流れ出る, 流れ込む ③ざあざあ降る
- **pray** 動 祈る, 懇願する
- **present** 動 贈る, 贈呈する
- **press** 動 押す 名 出版物[社], 新聞
- **price** 名 値段, 代価
- **princess** 名 王女 **Princess Ann** アン王女
- **private** 形 私的な, 個人の
- **problem** 名 問題, 難問
- **promise** 動 ①約束する ②見込みがある
- **pull** 動 ①引く, 引っ張る ②引きつける **pull away** 引き離す, もぎ取る **pull away from** ~から離れる **pull off** 離れる, 去る, (衣服などを)脱ぐ **pull out** 引き抜く, 引き出す, 取り出す **pull up** 引っ張り上げる
- **push** 動 ①押す, 押し進む, 押し進める ②進む, 突き出る **push away** 押しのける, 押しやる
- **put** 動 ①置く, のせる ②入れる, つける ③(ある状態に)する ④put の過去, 過去分詞 **put ~ into …** ~を…の状態にする, ~を…に突っ込む

- **put back** (もとの場所に)戻す, 返す
- **put in** 〜の中に入れる **put on** 〜を…の上に置く **put out** ①外に出す, (手など)を(差し)出す ②(明かり・火を)消す **put up** 〜を上げる, 揚げる, 建てる, 飾る

## Q

- **queen** 名 女王, 王妃
- **question** 名 質問, 疑問, 問題
- **quickly** 副 敏速に, 急いで
- **quiet** 形 静かな, 穏やかな, じっとした
- **quietly** 副 ①静かに ②平穏に, 控えめに
- **quite** 副 ①まったく, すっかり, 完全に ②かなり, ずいぶん ③ほとんど **not quite** まったく〜だというわけではない

## R

- **radio** 名 ラジオ
- **rain** 名 雨, 降雨 動 雨が降る
- **raise** 動 上げる
- **ran** 動 run(走る)の過去
- **rather** 副 ①むしろ, かえって ②かなり, いくぶん, やや ③それどころか逆に
- **reach** 動 ①着く, 到着する, 届く ②手を伸ばして取る
- **read** 動 読む, 読書する
- **ready** 形 用意[準備]ができた, まさに〜しようとする, 今にも〜せんばかりの **be ready for** 準備が整って, 〜に期待する **get ready** 用意[支度]をする **ready to go** すっかり準備が整った
- **real** 形 実際の, 実在する, 本物の
- **realize** 動 理解する, 実現する
- **really** 副 本当に, 実際に, 確かに
- **reason** 名 理由
- **relation** 名 (利害)関係, 間柄
- **remember** 動 思い出す, 覚えている, 忘れないでいる
- **remind** 動 思い出させる, 気づかせる
- **remove** 動 取り去る, 除去する
- **reporter** 名 レポーター, 報告者, 記者
- **rest** 名 ①休息 ②安静 ③休止, 停止 ④《the –》残り 動 ①休む, 眠る ②休止する, 静止する ③(〜に)基づいている ④(〜の)ままである **come to rest on** 〜のところで止まる
- **restaurant** 名 レストラン, 料理店, 食堂
- **rich** 形 ①富んだ, 金持ちの ②豊かな, 濃い, 深い
- **ride** 動 乗る, 乗って行く
- **right** 形 ①正しい ②適切な ③健全な ④右(側)の 副 ①まっすぐに, すぐに ②右(側)に ③ちょうど, 正確に **all right** 大丈夫で, よろしい, 申し分ない, わかった, 承知した **right now** 今すぐに, たった今
- **river** 名 川
- **road** 名 道路, 道, 通り
- **Rocca's** 名 ロッカズ《レストラン名》
- **rock** 名 岩, 岸壁, 岩石
- **rode** 動 ride(乗る)の過去
- **roll** 動 ①転がる, 転がす ②(波などが)うねる, 横揺れする 名 ①一巻き ②名簿, 目録 **drum roll** ドラムの連打
- **Roman** 形 ローマ(人)の
- **Rome** 名 ローマ《イタリアの首都》
- **room** 名 ①部屋 ②空間, 余地
- **rope** 名 綱, なわ, ロープ
- **row** 名 (横に並んだ)列
- **royal** 形 王の, 女王の, 国立の

# ROMAN HOLIDAY

- **royal official** 王室関係者
- **rub** 動 ①こする, こすって磨く ②すりむく
- **ruin** 形 台無しになった
- **run** 動 ①走る run across 走って渡る run after 〜を追いかける run away 走り去る, 逃げ出す run away from 〜から逃れる run into 〜に駆け込む, 〜の中に走って入る run over to 〜へ急いでやってくる, ひと走りする run up 〜に走り寄る 名 走ること
- **rush** 動 突進する, せき立てる 名 突進, 突撃, 殺到

## S

- **sad** 形 ①悲しい, 悲しげな ②惨めな, 不運な
- **sadly** 副 悲しそうに, 不幸にも
- **sadness** 名 悲しみ, 悲哀
- **safety** 名 安全, 無事, 確実
- **said** 動 say（言う）の過去, 過去分詞
- **Saint Angelo** サンタンジェロ《地名》
- **salary** 名 給料
- **same** 形 ①同じ, 同様の ②前述の 代《the-》同一の人[物]
- **sat** 動 sit（座る）の過去, 過去分詞
- **saw** 動 see（見る）の過去
- **say** 動 言う, 口に出す
- **scene** 名 光景, 風景
- **school** 名 学校
- **scooter** 名 ①スクーター《片足で地面をけりながら乗る遊具》②（原動機付き）スクーター
- **scream** 名 金切り声, 絶叫 動 叫ぶ, 金切り声を出す
- **search** 動 捜し求める, 調べる
- **second** 形 第2の, 2番の
- **secret** 形 ①秘密の, 隠れた ②神秘の, 不思議な 名 秘密, 神秘
- **secret service** シークレットサービス
- **secretary** 名 秘書
- **see** 動 ①見る, 見える, 見物する ②（〜と）わかる, 認識する, 経験する ③会う ④考える, 確かめる, 調べる ⑤気をつける you see あのね, いいですか
- **seem** 動（〜に）見える,（〜のように）思われる
- **sell** 動 売る, 売っている, 売れる
- **send** 動 ①送る, 届ける ②手紙を出す ③（人を〜に）行かせる ④《− + 人[物など] + 〜ing》〜を（ある状態に）する
- **sense** 名 ①感覚, 感じ ②《-s》意識, 正気, 本性 ③常識, 分別, センス ④意味 make sense 意味をなす, よくわかる
- **separate** 動 ①分ける, 分かれる, 隔てる 形 分かれた, 別れた, 別々の
- **serious** 形 ①まじめな, 真剣な ②重大な, 深刻な,（病気などが）重い
- **service** 名 secret service シークレットサービス
- **several** 形 ①いくつかの ②めいめいの
- **sew** 動 縫い物をする, 縫い付ける
- **shake** 動 振る shake one's hand (人)と握手をする
- **shall** 助 ①《I が主語で》〜するだろう, 〜だろう ②《I 以外が主語で》（…に）〜させよう,（…は）〜することになるだろう Shall I 〜?（私が）〜しましょうか。 Shall we 〜?（一緒に）〜しましょうか。
- **share** 動 分配する, 共有する
- **she** 代 彼女は[が]
- **shirt** 名 ワイシャツ, ブラウス
- **shock** 名 衝撃, ショック
- **shocked** 形 ショックを受けて, 驚いて

## Word List

- **shoe** 名《-s》靴
- **shoe shop** 靴屋
- **shook** 動 shake（振る）の過去
- **shop** 名店, 小売り店
- **short** 形短い
- **shot** 名皮下注射 **give someone a shot**（人）に注射をする
- **should** 助〜すべきである, 〜したほうがよい
- **shoulder** 名肩
- **show** 動①見せる, 示す, 見える ②明らかにする, 教える ③案内する
- **shut** 動①閉まる, 閉める, 閉じる ②たたむ ③閉じ込める ④shutの過去, 過去分詞
- **shy** 形内気な, 恥ずかしがりの, 臆病な
- **sick** 形①病気の ②むかついて, いや気がさして
- **side** 名側, 横, そば, 斜面 **either side of** 〜の両側に **from side to side** 左右に **on either side** 両側に
- **sidewalk** 名歩道
- **sight** 名光景, 眺め
- **sign** 名①きざし, 徴候 ②跡 ③記号 ④合図, 看板
- **simple** 形単純な, 簡単な, 質素な
- **since** 前〜以来 副それ以来
- **sir** 名あなた《目上の男性, 客などに対する呼びかけ》
- **sit** 動座る, 腰掛ける **sit up** 起き上がる, 上半身を起こす
- **sky** 名①空, 天空, 大空 ②天気, 空模様, 気候
- **sleep** 動①眠る, 寝る ②活動しない **sleep in** 寝床に入る, 朝寝坊する, 住み込む
- **sleeping** 形眠っている
- **sleepy** 形①眠い, 眠そうな ②活気のない
- **sleeve** 名袖, たもと, スリーブ
- **slow** 形遅い 動遅くする, 速度を落とす **slow down** 速度を落とす
- **slowly** 副遅く, ゆっくり
- **small** 形①小さい, 少ない ②取るに足りない
- **smile** 動微笑する, にっこり笑う **smile at** 〜に微笑みかける 名微笑, ほほえみ
- **smiling** 形ほほ笑んでいる
- **Smith** 名スミス《人名》
- **Smithy** 名スミシー《人名, スミスの愛称》
- **smoke** 動喫煙する, 煙を出す
- **so** 副①とても ②同様に, 〜もまた ③《先行する句・節の代用》そのように, そう **so 〜 as to …** …するほど〜で **so 〜 that …** 非常に〜なので… **so many** 非常に多くの 接①だから, それで ②では, さて
- **softly** 副柔らかに, 優しく, そっと
- **some** 形①いくつかの, 多少の ②ある, 誰か, 何か **some time** いつか, そのうち 代①いくつか ②ある人[物]たち
- **something** 代①ある物, 何か ②いくぶん, 多少
- **song** 名歌, 詩歌
- **soon** 副まもなく, すぐに, すみやかに **as soon as** 〜するとすぐ, 〜するや否や
- **sorry** 形気の毒に[申し訳なく]思う, 残念な
- **sort** 名種類, 品質 **a sort of** 〜のようなもの, 一種の〜
- **sound** 名音, 騒音, 響き, サウンド 動①音がする, 鳴る ②（〜のように）思われる,（〜と）聞こえる **sound like** 〜のように聞こえる
- **Spanish Steps** スペイン階段《スペイン広場にある階段》
- **speak** 動話す, 言う, 演説する
- **special** 形①特別の, 特殊の, 臨時の ②専門の

## Roman Holiday

- □ **spent** 動 spend（使う）の過去, 過去分詞
- □ **spoke** 動 speak（話す）の過去
- □ **spread** 動 広がる, 広げる **spread out** 広げる, 展開する
- □ **stage** 名 舞台
- □ **stair** 名《-s》階段
- □ **stand** 動 立つ, 立たせる, 立っている, ある **stand by** そばに立つ, 傍観する, 待機する **stand still** じっと立っている **stand up** 立ち上がる
- □ **start** 動 出発する, 始まる, 始める **start doing** ～し始める **start to do** ～し始める
- □ **station** 名 **police station** 警察署
- □ **stay** 動 ①とどまる, 泊まる, 滞在する ②持続する,（～の）ままでいる **stay in** 家にいる,（場所）に泊まる, 滞在する
- □ **step** 名 ①歩み, 1歩（の距離）②段階 ③踏み段, 階段 動 歩む, 踏む **step out** 外へ出る
- □ **Stephen Hausen** スティーヴン・ハウゼン《人名》
- □ **still** 副 ①まだ, 今でも ②それでも（なお）形 静止した, 静かな **stand still** じっと立っている
- □ **stone** 名 石, 小石 形 石の, 石製の
- □ **stood** 動 stand（立つ）の過去, 過去分詞
- □ **stop** 動 ①やめる, やめさせる, 止める, 止まる ②立ち止まる **stop doing** ～するのをやめる **stop to ～** しようと立ち止まる
- □ **story** 名 ①物語, 話 ②（建物の）階
- □ **strange** 形 ①知らない, 見［聞き］慣れない ②奇妙な, 変わった
- □ **street** 名 ①街路 ②《S-》～通り
- □ **strong** 形 ①強い, 堅固な, 強烈な ②濃い ③得意な
- □ **struck** 動 strike（打つ）の過去, 過去分詞
- □ **subject** 名 話題, 議題, 主題

- □ **such** 形 ①そのような, このような ②そんなに, とても, 非常に **such a** そのような
- □ **sudden** 名 **all of a sudden** 突然, 前触れもなしに
- □ **suddenly** 副 突然, 急に
- □ **suit** 名 スーツ, 背広
- □ **suppose** 動 ①仮定する, 推測する ②《be -d to ～》～することになっている, ～するものである
- □ **sure** 形 確かな, 確実な,《be - to ～》必ず［きっと］～する, 確信して **make sure** 確かめる, 確認する 副 確かに, まったく, 本当に
- □ **surely** 副 確かに, きっと
- □ **surprise** 動 驚かす, 不意に襲う 名 驚き, 不意打ち
- □ **surprised** 動 surprise（驚かす）の過去, 過去分詞 形 驚いた
- □ **swam** 動 swim（泳ぐ）の過去

## T

- □ **table** 名 テーブル, 食卓, 台
- □ **take** 動 ①取る, 持つ ②持って［連れて］いく, 捕らえる ③乗る ④（時間・労力を）費やす, 必要とする ⑤（ある動作を）する ⑥飲む ⑦耐える, 受け入れる **take a bath** 風呂に入る **take a picture** 写真を撮る **take care of** ～の世話をする, ～面倒を見る, ～を管理する **take off**（衣服を）脱ぐ **take out** 取り出す **take out of** ～から出す **take someone home**（人）を家まで送る **take up** 取り上げる
- □ **taken** 動 take（取る）の過去分詞
- □ **talk** 動 話す, 語る, 相談する
- □ **tall** 形 高い, 背の高い
- □ **taxi** 名 タクシー
- □ **tear** 名 涙
- □ **telegraph** 名 電報, 電信

## WORD LIST

- **telephone** 名電話, 電話機
- **tell** 動①話す, 言う, 語る ②教える, 知らせる, 伝える ③わかる, 見分ける **tell ~ to …** ~に…するように言う
- **temperature** 名温度, 体温
- **terrible** 形恐ろしい, ひどい, ものすごい, つらい
- **than** 接~よりも, ~以上に
- **thank** 動感謝する, 礼を言う **thank ~ for …** ~に対して礼を言う 名《-s》感謝, 謝意
- **that** 形その, あの 代①それ, あれ, その[あの]人[物] ②《関係代名詞》~である… **after that** その後 **That's it.** それだけのことだ。 **this way and that** あちこちへ, あの手この手で 接~ということ, ~なので, ~だから **so ~ that …** 非常に~なので… 副そんなに, それほど
- **the** 冠①その, あの ②《形容詞の前で》~な人々 副《- +比較級, - +比較級》~すればするほど…
- **their** 代彼(女)らの, それらの
- **them** 代彼(女)らを[に], それらを[に]
- **then** 副その時(に・は), それから, 次に **just then** そのとたんに 形その当時の
- **there** 副①そこに[で・の], そこへ, あそこへ ②《- is [are] ~》~がある[いる] **down there** 下の方で[に] **there is no way** ~する見込みはない
- **these** 代これら, これ 形これらの, この
- **they** 代①彼(女)らは[が], それらは[が] ②(一般の)人々は[が]
- **thing** 名①物, 事 ②《-s》事情, 事柄 ③《one's -s》持ち物, 身の回り品 ④人, やつ
- **think** 動思う, 考える **think highly of** ~を高く評価する, 尊敬する **think of** ~のことを考える, ~を思いつく, 考え出す
- **thirty** 名30(の数字), 30人[個] 形30の, 30人[個]の
- **this** 形①この, こちらの, これを ②今の, 現在の **this one** これ, こちら **this way and that** あちこちへ, あの手この手で **this way** このように 代①それ, この人[物] ②今, ここ **like this** このような, こんなふうに
- **those** 形それらの, あれらの 代それら[あれら]の人[物]
- **though** 接①~にもかかわらず, ~だが ②たとえ~でも **even though** ~であるけれども, ~にもかかわらず 副しかし
- **thought** 動 think (思う) の過去, 過去分詞
- **thousand** 名①1000(の数字), 1000人[個] ②《-s》何千, 多数 形①1000の, 1000人[個]の ②多数の
- **three** 名3(の数字), 3人[個] 形3の, 3人[個]の
- **threw** 動 throw (投げる) の過去
- **through** 前~を通して, ~中を[に], ~中
- **throw** 動投げる, 浴びせる, ひっかける **throw down** 投げ出す, 放棄する **throw up** 跳ね上げる
- **ticket** 名切符, 乗車[入場]券, チケット
- **tightly** 副きつく, しっかり, 堅く
- **time** 名①時, 時間, 歳月 ②時期 ③期間 ④時代 ⑤回, 倍 **all the time** ずっと, いつも, その間ずっと **at this time** 現時点では, このとき **for the first time** 初めて **just in time** いよいよというときに, すんでのところで, やっと間に合って **on time** 時間どおりに **some time** いつか, そのうち
- **tired** 形①疲れた, くたびれた ②あきた, うんざりした

- **title** 名題名, タイトル
- **to** 前①《方向・変化》~へ, ~に, ~の方へ ②《程度・時間》~まで ③《適合・付加・所属》~に ④《-+動詞の原形》~するために[の], ~する, ~すること
- **today** 名今日 副今日(で)は
- **toe** 名足指, つま先
- **together** 副①一緒に, ともに ②同時に
- **told** 動 tell（話す）の過去, 過去分詞
- **tomorrow** 名明日 副明日は
- **tonight** 名今夜, 今晩 副今夜は
- **too** 副①~も(また) ②あまりに~すぎる, とても~ **too ~ to …** …するには~すぎる **too much** 過度の
- **took** 動 take（取る）の過去
- **top** 名頂上, 首位 形いちばん上の
- **tour** 名ツアー, 見て回ること, 視察
- **toward** 前①《運動の方向・位置》~の方へ, ~に向かって ②《目的》~のために
- **towel** 名タオル
- **town** 名町, 都会, 都市
- **trade** 名取引, 貿易, 商業
- **traffic** 名通行, 往来, 交通(量), 貿易
- **travel** 動①旅行する ②進む, 移動する[させる], 伝わる
- **tray** 名盆, 盛り皿
- **trip** 動~をつまずかせる, 転ばせる
- **trouble** 名①困難, 迷惑 ②心配, 苦労 ③もめごと
- **truck** 名トラック, 運搬車
- **true** 形①本当の, 本物の, 真の ②誠実な, 確かな **come true** 実現する
- **truth** 名①真理, 事実, 本当 ②誠実, 忠実さ **Mouth of Truth** 真実の口《ローマの大きな人面の口》
- **try** 動①やってみる, 試みる ②努力する, 努める **try on** 試着してみる
- **turn** 動①ひっくり返す, 回転する[させる], 曲がる, 曲げる, 向かう, 向ける ②(~に)なる, (~に)変える **turn around** 振り向く, 向きを変える, 方向転換する **turn away** 向こうへ行く, 追い払う, (顔を)そむける, 横を向く **turn into** ~に変わる **turn off** (照明などを)消す **turn on** (スイッチなどを)ひねってつける, 出す **turn to** ~の方を向く 名順番
- **twenty** 名20(の数字), 20人[個] 形20の, 20人[個]の
- **two** 名2(の数字), 2人[個] 形2の, 2人[個]の
- **two-thirty** 2時30分

## U

- **um** 間ううん, ううむ
- **under** 前①《位置》~の下[に] ②《状態》~を受けて, ~のもと ③《数量》~以下[未満]の, ~より下の
- **understand** 動理解する, わかる, ~を聞いて知っている
- **understood** 動 understand（理解する）の過去, 過去分詞
- **underwear** 名下着(類)
- **uneasy** 形不安な, 焦って
- **unselfish** 形わがままでない, 無欲な
- **until** 前~まで(ずっと) 接~の時まで, ~するまで
- **up** 副①上へ, 上がって, 北へ ②立って, 近づいて ③向上して, 増して **up to** ~まで, ~に至るまで, ~に匹敵して 前①~の上の(方)へ, 高い方へ ②(道)に沿って
- **us** 代私たちを[に]
- **use** 動①使う, 用いる ②費やす 名使用, 用途 **no use** 役に立たない, 用をなさない

## WORD LIST

## V

- **very** 副 とても, 非常に, まったく 形 本当の, きわめて, まさしくその
- **view** 名 眺め, 景色, 見晴らし
- **visit** 動 訪問する 名 訪問
- **voice** 名 ①声, 音声 ②意見, 発言権

## W

- **wait** 動 ①待つ, 《–for ～》～を待つ ②延ばす, 延ばせる, 遅らせる ③《–on [upon] ～》～に仕える, 給仕をする
- **waiter** 名 ウェイター, 給仕
- **wake** 動 ①目がさめる, 起きる, 起こす ②奮起する **wake up** 起きる, 目を覚ます
- **walk** 動 歩く, 歩かせる, 散歩する **walk along** (前へ)歩く, ～に沿って歩く **walk away** 立ち去る, 遠ざかる **walk off** 立ち去る **walk out of** ～から出る **walk out the door** ドアの外に出る, どこかに行く **walk over** ～の方に歩いていく **walk past** 通り過ぎる **walk to** ～まで歩いて行く **walk up** 歩み寄る, 歩いて上る **walk up to** ～に歩み寄る 名 歩くこと, 散歩
- **wall** 名 ①壁, 塀 ②障壁
- **want** 動 ほしい, 望む, ～したい, ～してほしい
- **war** 名 戦争(状態), 闘争, 不和
- **warm** 形 暖かい, 温暖な
- **was** 動 《beの第1・第3人称単現在am, isの過去》～であった, (～に)いた[あった]
- **wash** 動 洗う, 洗濯する
- **watch** 動 ①じっと見る, 見物する ②注意[用心]する, 監視する
- **water** 名 ①水 ②(川・湖・海などの) 多量の水
- **wave** 動 ①揺れる, 揺らす, 波立つ ②(手などを振って)合図する
- **way** 名 ①道, 通り道 ②方向, 距離 ③方法, 手段 ④習慣 **find one's way** たどり着く **in a way** ある意味では **make one's way** 進む, 行く, 成功する **there is no way** ～する見込みはない **this way** このように **this way and that** あちこちへ, あの手この手で
- **we** 代 私たちは[が]
- **weakly** 副 弱々しく
- **wear** 動 着る, 着ている, 身につける
- **week** 名 週, 1週間
- **well** 副 ①うまく, 上手に ②十分に, よく, かなり **as well** なお, その上, 同様に 間 へえ, まあ, ええと 形 健康な, 適当な, 申し分ない
- **went** 動 go (行く)の過去
- **were** 動 《beの2人称単数・複数の過去》～であった, (～に)いた[あった]
- **wet** 形 ぬれた, 湿った, 雨の 動 ぬらす, ぬれる
- **what** 代 ①何が[を・に] ②《関係代名詞》～するところのもの[こと] **what … for** どんな目的で **What (～) for?** 何のために, なぜ 形 ①何の, どんな ②なんと ③～するだけの 副 いかに, どれほど
- **when** 副 ①いつ ②《関係副詞》～するところの, ～するとその時, ～するとき 接 ～の時, ～するとき 代 いつ
- **whenever** 接 ①～するときはいつでも, ～するたびに ②いつ～しても
- **where** 副 ①どこに[で] ②《関係副詞》～するところの, そしてそこで, ～するところ **where to** どこで～すべきか 接 ～なところに[へ], ～するところに[へ] 代 ①どこ, どの点 ②～するところの

- **which** 形 ①どちらの, どの, どれでも ②どんな～でも, そしてこの 代 ①どちら, どれ, どの人[物] ②《関係代名詞》～するところの
- **while** 接 ①～の間(に), ～する間(に) ②一方, ～なのに 名 しばらくの間, 一定の時 **for a while** しばらくの間, 少しの間
- **who** 代 ①誰が[は], どの人 ②《関係代名詞》～するところの(人)
- **whole** 形 全体の, すべての, 完全な, 満～, 丸～ 名《the－》全体, 全部
- **whom** 代 ①誰を[に] ②《関係代名詞》～するところの人, そしてその人を
- **why** 副 ①なぜ, どうして ②《関係副詞》～するところの(理由) **Why don't you ～?** ～したらどうだい, ～しませんか。 **Why not?** どうしてだめなのですか。いいですとも。ぜひそうしよう！ 間 ①おや, まあ ②もちろん, なんだって ③ええと
- **wide** 副 広く, 大きく開いて
- **wildly** 副 荒々しく, 乱暴に, むやみに
- **will** 助 ～だろう, ～しよう, する(つもりだ) **Will you ～?** ～してくれませんか。
- **win** 動 勝つ, 獲得する, 達する
- **window** 名 窓, 窓ガラス
- **wine** 名 ワイン, ぶどう酒
- **wipe** 動 ～をふく, ぬぐう, ふきとる
- **wish** 動 望む, 願う, (～であればよいと)思う **wish for** 所望する 名 (心からの)願い
- **with** 前 ①《同伴・付随・所属》～と一緒に, ～を身につけて, ～とともに ②《様態》～(の状態)で, ～して ③《手段・道具》～で, ～を使って
- **without** 前 ～なしで, ～がなく, ～しないで
- **woke** 動 wake (目が覚める)の過去

- **woman** 名 (成人した)女性, 婦人
- **won** 動 win (勝つ)の過去, 過去分詞
- **won't** will notの短縮形
- **wonderful** 形 驚くべき, すばらしい, すてきな
- **word** 名 ①語, 単語 ②ひと言 ③《one's－》約束
- **wore** 動 wear (着ている)の過去
- **work** 動 働く 名 仕事 **get to work** 仕事にとりかかる
- **world** 名《the－》世界, ～界 **all over the world** 世界中に
- **worried** 形 心配そうな, 不安げな
- **worry** 動 悩む, 悩ませる, 心配する[させる] 名 苦労, 心配
- **worth** 形 (～の)価値がある, (～)しがいがある 名 価値, 値打ち
- **would** 助《willの過去》①～するだろう, ～するつもりだ ②～したものだ **would like to** ～したいと思う **Would you ～?** ～してくださいませんか。 **Would you like ～?** ～はいかがですか。
- **wow** 間《驚き, 喜び, 苦痛などを表して》わあ！, ああ！
- **write** 動 書く, 手紙を書く
- **writing** 動 write (書く)の現在分詞 名 書き物, 書かれたもの, 文書
- **wrong** 形 ①間違った, (道徳上)悪い ②調子が悪い, 故障した

## Y

- **yeah** 間 うん, そうだね
- **year** 名 ～歳
- **yell** 動 大声をあげる, わめく
- **yes** 間 はい, そうです
- **yesterday** 名 ①昨日 ②過ぎし日, 昨今 副 昨日(は)
- **yet** 副 ①《否定文で》まだ～(ない[し

ない]) ②《疑問文で》もう ③《肯定文で》まだ, 今もなお
- **you** 代 ①あなた(方)は[が], あなた(方)を[に] ②(一般に)人は **you know** ご存知のとおり, そうでしょう **you see** あのね, いいですか
- **young** 形 若い, 幼い, 青年の
- **your** 代 あなた(方)の **Your (Royal) Highness**《呼びかけ》殿下
- **yourself** 代 あなた自身

# E-CAT

## English Conversational Ability Test
国際英語会話能力検定

● E-CATとは…
英語が話せるようになるための
テストです。インターネット
ベースで、30分であなたの発
話力をチェックします。

www.ecatexam.com

# iTEP
Academic · Business · SLATE
International Test of English Proficiency

● iTEP®とは…
世界各国の企業、政府機関、アメリカの大学300校以上が、英語能力判定テストとして採用。オンラインによる90分のテストで文法、リーディング、リスニング、ライティング、スピーキングの5技能をスコア化。iTEP®は、留学、就職、海外赴任などに必要な、世界に通用する英語力を総合的に評価する画期的なテストです。

www.itepexamjapan.com

---

ラダーシリーズ

**Roman Holiday** ローマの休日

2011年2月7日　第1刷発行
2019年8月11日　第10刷発行

原著者　イアン・マクレラン・ハンター

発行者　浦　晋亮

発行所　IBCパブリッシング株式会社
　　　　〒162-0804 東京都新宿区中里町29番3号
　　　　菱秀神楽坂ビル9F
　　　　Tel. 03-3513-4511　Fax. 03-3513-4512
　　　　www.ibcpub.co.jp

---

© IBC Publishing, Inc. 2011

印　刷　株式会社シナノパブリッシングプレス
装　丁　伊藤 理恵
イラスト　菊地 玲奈
組版データ　ITC Berkeley Oldstyle Medium + ITC Berkeley Oldstyle Black

落丁本・乱丁本は、小社宛にお送りください。送料小社負担にてお取り替えいたします。本書の無断複写(コピー)は著作権法上での例外を除き禁じられています。

Printed in Japan
ISBN978-4-7946-0064-6